So All Can Learn

You make a
difference !

John
McCarthy

So All Can Learn

A Practical Guide to Differentiation

John McCarthy

ROWMAN & LITTLEFIELD
Lanham • Boulder • New York • London

Published by Rowman & Littlefield
A wholly owned subsidiary of The Rowman & Littlefield Publishing Group, Inc.
4501 Forbes Boulevard, Suite 200, Lanham, Maryland 20706
www.rowman.com

Unit A, Whitacre Mews, 26–34 Stannary Street, London SE11 4AB

British Library Cataloguing in Publication Information Available

Library of Congress Cataloging-in-Publication Data Is Available

ISBN 978-1-4758-2570-1 (cloth : alk. paper)
ISBN 978-1-4758-2571-8 (pbk. : alk. paper)
ISBN 978-1-4758-2572-5 (electronic)

♾™ The paper used in this publication meets the minimum requirements of American
National Standard for Information Sciences—Permanence of Paper for Printed Library
Materials, ANSI/NISO Z39.48–1992.

Printed in the United States of America

Contents

Foreword

For John McCarthy, Author

SO ALL CAN LEARN: A PRACTICAL GUIDE
TO DIFFERENTIATION

When someone writes about their passions, you can feel it come right off the pages. Add teachers and students into the mix, and you can feel the passion even deeper. When you are writing for your own children's success . . . well, you get the picture.

John McCarthy has been an educational leader in the area of differentiation for more than 20 years. He has worked in schools across the globe sharing his passion with teachers who are truly in it for the kids. Our paths crossed almost 20 years ago when we both started a leadership journey that taught us that we "lead from where we stand" and being advocates for our profession and students is what it is all about. John has exemplified this model in his new book . . . leading, modeling, and advocating for both teachers and students. Twenty plus years of experience and 1000s of classrooms later, John has captured the importance of differentiation and the empowerment it brings to classrooms.

Our paths again crossed at Wayne County RESA, Michigan's largest Regional Education Service Agency located right in the heart of Detroit. We both were school improvement consultants. Again, John embraced the idea of "leading from where you stand" by bringing differentiation to the forefront in Wayne County. He embraced the teacher and the student, improving and empowering one classroom, one school, and one district at a time. His passion led to professional learning and led him to join the Buck Institute for Education, and his travels began across the globe. His work in Wayne County began to cross state lines and then oceans as demands for speaking and talent for improving schools were beginning to be recognized. John demonstrated the power of differentiation in schools where multiple languages, cultures, and climates intersected in the Detroit area. He showed teachers and administrators alike that all students can learn by shaping the learning and strategies for learning to the individual.

I too began a journey of my own, to seek a new place to stand and lead. I found myself as a principal of an elementary school in an urban Michigan school district. The challenges were many. Decisions on whether to be a manager or a leader were before me. Instructional leader or business leader . . . my passions in the world of instruction were strong . . . an instructional leader it would be. My teachers were strong, leaders in their own right, and adventurous too! John joined me on this journey a few times to shadow me at my school. Our walks together in the halls, peeking into classrooms, and an occasional staff meeting led to great dialogue about instructional practices that make a difference. One of the conversations shows up in this book. ;) As a teacher I didn't read the CA-60 (student file that gets passed on year by year). I wanted to know my students from day one, not the days that lead them to my classroom door. I wanted to get to know their strengths and challenges, not by someone else's observations. Time had passed, growth may have occurred. Who knows their kids better than their parents? I asked the parents to write me a letter each year to tell me about their child's strengths and weaknesses, to tell me what gets them motivated, to inform me the best ways to communicate with their child and them as parents. As I shared with John and many others, I didn't always get 100% of the kids covered by these personal messages of growth and quite frankly awe . . . however, for the parents who took the time to inform me, I learned so much more, began a relationship so much stronger with both the student and the parents . . . far more than a file from the past describing where the student may or may not have been in that moment.

John has always been a learner and a writer! Ever since I have known him, he has been working on something. He met with his writers group, the Deadwood Writers, talked about the experience with me many times over lunch, and encouraged me to write. John is not only a talented writer but also a storyteller who can make the strategies come off the page. John's new book *So All CAN Learn: A Practical Guide to Differentiation* is filled with ideas for educators to "provide access to knowledge, skills, and concepts through a variety of delivery systems and instructional strategies." John explains, defines, and gives real examples that guide both the novice and seasoned teachers. His challenge is for "teachers to be working more efficiently and having students do all the heavy lifting of learning."

This book is resource rich and invites you to add to your own toolkits!

Syndee Malek, Ed.S.
Leadership Development Consultant

Preface

Differentiation has been my passion since my first day of teaching. I was filled with excitement and enthusiasm for the moment I became a third-generation teacher. Like my grandmother, and mother, before me, I wanted to make a difference in the world by supporting the next generations along their learning journey and preparing them for their future.

In American history, I told the students about the great time we'd have exploring history together. While I sought to convince them to be as enthusiastic as I felt, the students sat quietly in rows, staring at me. Near the end of the period, I gave them their first reading assignment, which I planned on using for an eventful Q&A (question and answer) session on Monday.

One of the students raised his hand. *Yes,* I enthused to myself, *my first student question of my career.* The young man spoke with firm politeness. "Mr. McCarthy, we don't do homework on the weekends. That's our time." The entire class nodded in agreement.

Every day that I teach and coach, that student's voice echoes in my head. He, and the many students who've followed him, reminds me that becoming a successful teacher means involving students in the teaching and learning processes, because they, not me, are in control of learning. Starting where students are in their understanding and perceptions, differentiation becomes just how learning happens. Developing my differentiation skills never stops.

THE DIFFERENTIATION CHALLENGE

Behind every person is a cadre of teachers who intersected their path. We've all heard that the profession of teaching is a calling. For many, there is a desire for meeting students' needs, helping them learn, and building their skills. Through time and effort, we strive to help them grow into someone more capable, confident, and learned so as to find success in their lives.

The responsibilities on teachers are great. Not all who answer the call are able to shoulder the responsibilities successfully, at least not without ongoing reflection and learning. Teachers must navigate the challenges of working with a group of individuals who have different perspectives about themselves, the tasks asked of them, and about the teacher. One constant is that each group of students will vary widely in their skills, personalities, and confidence. For these reasons alone, differentiation is imperative.

The reality is that differentiation happens. It may be part of a thoughtful plan or emerge from the need to modify instruction because some students have disengaged when they do not understand, a gap in skills is uncovered, or the content is already deeply known. Add to the mix the expectations by testing, instructional initiatives, political mandates, and public criticism, student learning can be lost in the fog. Yet the calling and responsibility remains: student learning.

This book, *So All Can Learn*, is intended to help teachers support themselves and mentor others on how to address that which they have control: their instructional work with students. Differentiation is a lens for meeting learner needs based on the instructional outcomes required of students. This same lens can be used to bridge mandates and challenges to meet student needs in the best ways that educators can design.

Often times, differentiation is misunderstood as something that cannot be done in "my situation." But if differentiation happens with or without our conscious intervention, then what is needed by teachers and administrators is how to frame and plan differentiation so that all can learn. Education professionals simply need an understanding of frameworks for how to differentiate effectively and more tools to support learning by all students.

PEDAGOGIES AND STRATEGIES

Through the many workshops and coaching experiences I have provided, every teacher I worked with believed that they taught students who:

- are composed of a mixture of skill levels
- learn at different rates and paces
- have unique personalities and perceptions

Yet, many of the teachers shared a common thought that differentiation is an ideal that is unattainable in the real world of the classroom. For those teachers to transform their view of differentiation to one of practical approaches, they needed understanding of concrete frameworks that work. They had to unpack the relationship of pedagogies and practices.

The term "differentiated instruction" represents a myriad of ideas about teaching and learning. Many teachers and administrators talk about it in terms of strategies that support instruction. For example, what are differentiated writing strategies or differentiated math strategies? This question creates an assumption that there are strategies that are labeled as differentiated, and those that are not. Any strategy can be differentiated for the needs of learners, but to be effective the pedagogical practices need to align with the purpose.

Pedagogies and strategies are the challenges that teachers struggle with when understanding and applying differentiation. Pedagogy is defined as:

> The method and practice of teaching, especially as an academic subject or theoretical concept. (*Oxford Dictionaries*)[1]

Strategy is defined as:

> A plan of action designed to achieve a long-term or overall aim. (*Oxford Dictionaries*)[2]

Unlike this book, most resources about differentiated instruction focus on one or the other. When pedagogy is explored, the response by teachers is "that sounds good, but how do I apply it in my classroom." When strategies are taught, they are presented as tools to implement, but no depth of context is provided as to the kinds of situation that are best applicable. A result is that teachers use the strategies in lessons that might not be the best fit for the learner or the intent of the learning. When this happens, differentiation is seen as a failure.

Successful differentiation happens when we approach teaching and learning based on understanding the existing strengths and challenges of each student. The more that is known about a student, and the more that students are invited to co-participate in their learning experiences, learning grows. Differentiation is not an elusive and unattainable ideal to be dreamt about in a *perfect world*. Differentiation is a way to provide teachers and other educators a lens on connecting pedagogy to existing effective instructional strategies and transform them to become more impactful for students.

HOW BEST TO USE *SO ALL CAN LEARN*

In this book, the approach mirrors my success with supporting teachers and administrators through workshops and coaching. Each chapter explores pedagogical concepts alongside practices. The examples in the chapters help to illustrate the ideas and are either actual usage by educators or a representation of various experiences that happened in different places of differentiation through my career and travels.

Each chapter includes a section at the end for reflection about pedagogy and opportunities to apply strategies within the reader's own work. This section will support the individual who seeks to find ways to improve or fine-tune their work with students, the study group at a school or district looking to develop common language and practice in their culture, and college courses for preservice teachers and graduate students who wish to be better prepared to meet the needs of their students on day one, rather than feeling underwater and at-risk of burnout within the first three years of the profession.

The book can be read sequentially or explore the chapters in any order that supports your needs, and those of your colleagues and students.

FINAL THOUGHTS FOR TAKING THIS JOURNEY

Differentiation is a necessary part of helping learners grow. It is my belief and hope that this book contributes to empowering educators to develop or grow their practice for meeting needs of all their students. This book, like myself, is not *the* fountain of knowledge for differentiation. Reading the chapters should reflect already-held beliefs about good teaching and learning practices. Readers will hopefully find themselves connecting their own valuable experiences with the ideas, frameworks, and examples that reaffirm their own practice, ignite new or different approaches to teaching and learning, and raise questions about one's classroom, school, or district culture.

Please contact me with your observations, reflections, and questions at jmccarthyeds@gmail.com, @jmccarthyeds on Twitter, or on my website: www.SoAllCanLearn.org. I welcome your thinking as an opportunity to expand my own perspectives.

As you read this book, *So All Can Learn,* I invite you to seek out the student voices from your own experiences, as I have from my first day of teaching. May this book help you find ways to adequately respond to *their* needs.

Acknowledgments

Writing may be a lonely endeavor, but the making of this book required the helping hands of many travelers. The ideas and formulation of strategies and other implementation were born of much work in classrooms, interactions with other educators, study, and conversations. Many times, I sat with other teachers and talked about how education would be better for students if . . . Inspired by those conversations and the efforts of educators working with students, I've finally placed the words to the page. There are many people I need to thank, but will likely not name them all with limited space and memory for names. But, my appreciation runs deep.

I wish to first thank those who mentored me, graciously and unselfishly giving of their experience and time to shine light on paths I could take to grow. Professor Jere Holman took me under his wing in graduate school, and gifted me with the power of ethnography and renewed purpose as a teacher. Hellen Stanks charged me with the task of providing coaching on differentiated instruction to the largest county in Michigan, and backed me with all the resources to succeed. David Ross opened a door to working with schools across the country, thus expanding my understanding of instructional practices and the people who do the work every day. His advice helped make this a better book. Susan Allan gave me profound insights into differentiated instruction from a 10,000-foot view to the classroom-level view, which continues to influence my practice. I am forever grateful.

I thank my professional learning networks for constantly challenging me to learn, grow, shifting my thinking, and to never be content with current success. There are many on this list, and I would name Syndee Malek, Beth Rayl, Myla Lee, Dayna Laur, Michael Gorman, and Amos Fodchuck. The Deadwood Writer's Group provides ongoing support in my writing journey and has helped me find my writing voice and strengthen my author craft. The best writer's group ever (www.deadwoodwriters.org).

I deeply appreciate the educators who when I asked to use their examples and words in this book said yes without hesitation. This book is richer because of their contributions. Their names appear in the book next to their work.

Special thanks goes to Kathy McCarthy, my wife, who not only encouraged and supported me as I wrote this book, but she also read and critiqued it. If anything is unclear in the book, it is my responsibility for not doing a good enough revision based on her advice. I thank Claire Murray for proofreading and clearing up all the grammatical errors that I'd passed off as writing creatively. I also thank Beth Rayl for her help with edits. Equally important on this team, I appreciate my editor, Sarah Jubar, who read my many blog posts and saw possibility for sharing a deeper version of my message about differentiation and student voice. Without her belief, advocacy, and patience, this book does not exist.

Most important, I thank my children, Dagan and Jada, who remind me every day the impact of education when differentiation is used and ignored. Every support I desired or advocated for them to grow is deserving to all students.

And, thank you reader for choosing to join me on this journey for improving practice of differentiation. I hope that you'll dialogue with me through the book and social media. We share the common interest of providing practical differentiation so *all* can learn.

NOTES

1. Pedagogy: *Oxford Dictionaries*. https://en.oxforddictionaries.com/definition/pedagogy.
2. Strategies: *Oxford Dictionaries*. https://en.oxforddictionaries.com/definition/strategy.

Chapter 1

What Is Differentiation, Really?

> DI seems so much less overwhelming when one realizes they already differentiate the content as you've described. I realize I don't give my students enough time to process the content as I should, and am looking forward to implementing your suggestions such as Think-Pair-Share, Journaling, Partner talk, and Save the Last Word.
>
> —Kathy Coker[1]

Every school year is challenging. The task of taking students on day one toward learning a course worth of curriculum by the end of the year seems like a monumental task. An example is one teacher's journey with high school sophomores. English second year was one of the three preps that Mr. John taught. He was charged with the task of developing writing skills in three areas—informational, narrative, and persuasive—raising reading levels, building research skills, using various communication formats, and applying grammar and mechanics. Those were just the major topics, which represented a multitude of skills and concepts.

To make the challenge more difficult, Mr. John's students were not all at the same skill level. He had students who either *hated* to write or were indifferent to the extent that they put minimal effort into the practice. Also, one student was a talented writer beyond her nearest peer.

The teacher announced on the first day that all students would publish writing at least once every 10 weeks. He hoped to aim high and show the students that their ideas mattered. The response surprised him. Half the students groaned, while a few put their heads down. One student politely asked for a pass to the counselor's office.

As the pass was being written, the student explained his intentions to drop the class. The student was terrified of everyone seeing how poor of a writer he was through publication. That's when Mr. John realized how challenging the year would be. He convinced that student to give him, the teacher, a 10-week trial. See how the experience went. The student would decide when something of his was published. The student agreed. One down, a whole class of students left to convince.

The task of getting student buy-in and developing writing skills required a lot of hard work, risks, failures, disappointments, time, and lots of patience. Mr. John broke down writing into various parts to help students understand the mechanics and structures. He used strategies such as one-foot voice, fast write-free write, portrait writing, inference riddles, choice and voice, and rubrics[2]—just in the area of writing. Students did publish work on the classroom website and sent submissions to outside publications. The first student to have a submission accepted for publication was the young man who on the first day had wanted to transfer out of the class.

Because of differentiation, Mr. John succeeded in that *most* of his students did improve as writers. Also, *most* did develop the English skills in all of the required areas. However, there were students who were not successful, and there were some students who did not grow enough because they were never sufficiently challenged.

THE CHALLENGE AND PROMISE OF DIFFERENTIATION

Mr. John's story illustrates what makes each school year challenging for teachers. Like Sisyphus,[3] who rolls a boulder up a hill only to have it roll back down and has to repeat the backbreaking process again, teachers must take on the annual challenge of guiding their charges to *all* successfully complete the school year. Unlike Sisyphus, who is doomed to repeat his task for eternity, there is a hope and possibility for a teacher to shepherd all of her students to achieve academically at the appropriate levels: informed differentiation so all can learn.

Introduce the Challenge and Promise of Differentiation

Time, pacing charts, proscriptive curriculum, mandates, and standardized testing are commonly shared as the major challenges to instructing students, much less differentiation. Yet, these are all symptoms of a greater obstacle that prevents teachers and administrators from addressing student learning: themselves.

What's ironic is that this obstacle is also the only hope of students having success. When tasked with finding ways to overcome the challenges that threaten students' success, educators find ways to open paths so that learners grow. They understand that the profession of educators is to develop the succeeding generations to be better than ourselves. This is especially critical because each generation taught by current teachers will eventually replace us as the caretakers for the world—and us. How do we find solutions to these problems? One possible answer: Differentiation becomes the key for educators to reclaim the high ground for ensuring that all students can learn?

LENS ON LEARNING

Often, differentiation is understood as a collection of strategies that are used to meet the needs of different learners. This viewpoint is at best shortsighted. At worst, it's a misunderstanding that leads to limited instructional successes that causes much of the clamor that differentiation works only in a *perfect* world. This frustration is understandable because dialogue about differentiation looks at either pedagogy or strategies, with not enough connections made between the two.

The differentiation lens is the frame for how teachers can find means to enhance or adapt their pedagogy for delivering instruction. It is also how teachers can determine what strategies will be most effective for actual implementation of lessons. The differentiation lens is like a high-quality camera lens that can be attached to any pedagogy and used to zoom in for individual needs of some learners. Other times, the lens is pulled back to look at the big picture of curriculum frameworks and state or national standards.

The differentiation lens zooms in and out with gradual lens adjustments to focus on specific interventions that are intended to provide a structure for school-wide or curriculum-wide instruction such as STEM/STEAM Understanding by Design, Assessments for Learning, Project or Inquiry-Based Learning, College & Career-Readiness Skills, Restorative Practices, Response to Intervention, Universal Design for Learning, and Authentic Learning Experiences. Under these umbrella initiatives, teachers further narrow the lens using student formative assessment data to plan instruction so that all can learn.

Differentiation is a lens used at all education levels and ages. Teachers use the differentiation lens when planning and implementing learning experiences that target the specific needs of their learners. Using a variety of student assessment data, both academic and personal, teachers structure a range of powerful learning experiences for whole class, small groups, and individuals.

The differentiation lens works under any climate or system, no matter the latest initiative, curriculum review, school improvement initiative, or top-down mandate. From the most open environment to the most restrictive environment, the differentiation lens is a necessary step for planning,

implementing, and assessing learner outcomes. Why? The educators' job is
to provide support so that all can learn.

Common Language for Differentiation

Planning and implementation is based on a framework of differentiation elements developed by such pioneers as Carol Ann Tomlinson, Ph.D., and Susan Allan, Ph.D.

- Content
- Process
- Products
- Readiness
- Interests
- Learning preferences

How these elements are used determines the effectiveness of the learning experiences for students. It is important to have some historical context of differentiation, so that the importance and value of these elements can be best understood and used.

A History of Modern Differentiation

In 1999, Carol Tomlinson published *The Differentiated Classroom: Responding to the Needs of All Learners* by Association for Supervision and Curriculum Development (ASCD). It laid out an argument for the importance of getting to know the whole student and for teachers to incorporate what they learned into lessons so that all could learn. A year later, Susan Allan coauthored with Carol Tomlinson the book *Leadership for Differentiating Schools & Classrooms*. Both books provided an early view of "A Concept Map for Differentiating Instruction," which is shared widely across the world.

In 2001, Carol Tomlinson wrote the book *How to Differentiate Instruction in Mixed-Ability Classrooms*. It further explained these concepts, committing a chapter to each. Since this breakout book, there have been many authors who focus on these ideas as separate subjects that any teacher can use in his or her instruction. However, this approach misses the core ideas of the concepts.

In *Fulfilling the Promise of the Differentiated Classroom* (2003), Carol Tomlinson explained a relationship of differentiation and pedagogy with her Three Cogs for Differentiation, which raised new and important ideas about the interrelationship of students, teachers, and curriculum. She dedicated a chapter to each on the roles of students and teachers, and two chapters on curriculum. As of this printing, there have been authors who came close to addressing these important connections for differentiation's place in pedagogy, but none has matched or furthered those ideas.

This is not to diminish the many books available on differentiation. Since these books' publication, there are many good texts, articles, and media that address different subjects regarding differentiation, such as grading and assessment practices, literacy, numeracy, management, brain-related research, and other strategies.

More dialogue is needed on the connections between pedagogy and application that originates with the students' perspective and teacher's planning and coaching. That conversation occurs here by building from the common language established by pioneers of DI like Carol Tomlinson and Susan Allan.

THE DIFFERENTIATION RELATIONSHIP

Think about a student who struggled in class. Every teacher has several on his or her roster. They are the ones who resist help. In fact, they put so much energy into fighting against the offered support that the teacher might wish to say, "If you would just use that energy for good and accept my support, you could learn so much."

This occurrence represents the interrelationship of the work of teachers and the choices made by students. Teachers who plan and implement instruction without considering students' viewpoints regarding the course and the work face an incredibly difficult, some might say impossible, task of having all of their students achieve academically. For example, consider when individuals attend a meeting or professional development where the feeling is that the instructor or plan was out of touch with the participants' needs. Many will tend to disconnect or pay lip service until the session ends. As participants exit the room, they do info-dumps, remembering nothing of value.

The elements do not represent a pedagogy or list of tools. When used in isolation, the results lead to questionable learning. The interrelationship shines a light on how differentiation connects teacher practice—content, process, and product—is influenced by how students respond—readiness, interests, and learning preferences.

Teacher instructional planning and student responses determine learning successes and failures. The cycling nature of the reflective process happens best when teachers consider data on what students need, how they might respond, and ways to include them in decision-making. This process, referred to as student voice, is a collaboration of teacher and learners, which is addressed more deeply in Chapter 6. Let's explore the key elements of differentiation for a clearer understanding of this cycle of this reflective process.

The Learner Relationship

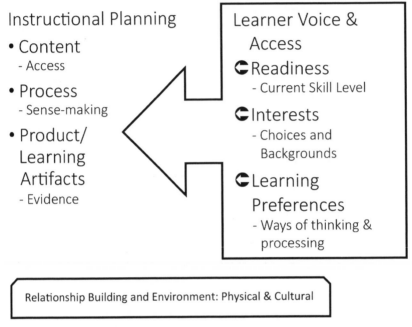

Figure 1.1.   The Learner Relationship

CORE DIFFERENTIATION LANGUAGE EXPLAINED

The language of differentiation is composed of eight elements. Based on the work by Carol Tomlinson, Susan Allan, and other pioneers, these elements are interdependent in practice. To understand their relationship, what follows are explanations of the elements from different perspectives. The format is like the Frayer Model unboxed. Read and reflect how the meaning for each best presents itself for you.

Instructional Planning

1. CONTENT

DEFINE:

Provide access to knowledge, skills, and concepts through a variety of delivery systems and instructional strategies. Content is what students need to develop a level of achievement or mastery. Carol Ann Tomlinson in some of her presentations and writings uses the term "KUD," or what students need to know, understand, and do.[4]

RATIONALE:

One delivery approach does not make sense to all learners. A lecture, research, video, or reading is less effective as solitary communication modes. Provide students with a combination of content delivery so that they are engaged from multiple perspectives. This ensures that all learners are more likely to make connections by drawing from the variety of communication.

LEARNER CONNECTION:

Every educator knows from experience that any group of students may vary widely in skills and level of understanding of content. Content delivery should factor readiness levels, sometimes providing content to students grouped with similar skills, such as guided reading. With groups of mixed-skill levels, from small to whole class, content may be provided through tasks that include scaffolds for those in need, so that they can better understand the work.

Learning preferences play a key role when content is delivered in multiple ways to ensure that all students can find success. Use strategies like videos, discussions, readings, and visuals to give learners a variety of ways to connect. Learners will find that at least some of the displays of content make sense, which would not happen if only one mode of delivery is used.

Interests are useful in showing how content is reflected in familiar areas to the learner. It is not unusual for teachers to craft a lesson around the interests of a few students. If they cannot relate to the curriculum they may tune out and fall further behind.

EXAMPLES:

- Students are studying *To Kill a Mockingbird*. While reading assigned chapters, students have the option to listen to an audio recording while following along in the book.
- Students read an article using the "Save the Last Word for Me" protocol. The reading is chunked into two or three sections. Students discuss each part to check for understanding. They then read the next section and repeat the process.
- The students from three classes are grouped by readiness for math-skill level. Each teacher takes a group and works with them at their appropriate level. Even so, the teachers use a variety of centers based on interest and

learning preferences to ensure that learners make connections beyond the abstract level of the math concepts.

• Elementary students are grouped by reading level for guided reading. They read text at their appropriate instructional need. Students who demonstrate readiness to move to a higher-reading level are moved to that group. Other individual learners who struggle in one group can join another that meets their needs. In this way, groups are fluid. This avoids static groups where once assigned, a student remains for the entire year.

2. PROCESS

DEFINE:

Develop and structure opportunities for learners to make sense of content or check for understanding before and after content delivery and activities, such as assignments. Ongoing formative assessments can play an important role when students pause in instruction to process the content delivered.

RATIONALE:

Process is about checking for learner understanding before moving on with a lesson or starting an assignment. It's important for students and teachers to know if any support is needed before making a transition. Some have viewed process as the structures that teachers use to make learning more conducive for students. While this occurs, student understanding should be the center of the focus. When content is delivered in various formats and approaches, checking for understanding is critical. What students know and do not know is at the core for how instruction evolves. Consider processing activities as informative assessments done by students to check for their understanding.

LEARNER CONNECTION:

Having visited many classrooms across the United States, the learning experiences tend to follow a similar sequence. The teacher provides instruction for content acquisition, which can take many forms—see the Content section discussed earlier—and then students are assigned a task to complete. This task may be intended for practice or formative assessment.

What can be frustrating is that students do not get an opportunity to check that they understood the content before doing the assignment. Taking five minutes to do a processing activity can allow students to realize any gaps in their understanding or misperceptions before diving into a meaty assignment.

Sure, some assignments are structured as small group or independent tasks that allow teachers to provide individual coaching. Yet, imagine how the third or fourth student waiting for his or her turns feels. Frustration that shuts them down can be avoided through a processing experience. The result may require reteaching to the whole group or breakout mini lessons for smaller groups as needed.

EXAMPLES:

- Students read primary source documents using the "Three Levels of Text" protocol. Student groups chunk the document for reading. For each section, they delve deeply through dialogue about the content and its implications.
- About every five to ten minutes during a presentation, the students did written and oral reflections based on prompts. The teacher moved around the students to listen in on their thinking, while other times randomly selecting student groups to share ideas from their conversations.
- Before starting the practice work, students completed an exit card. In another class, students completed a quick survey using remotes or computers. In both cases, the teachers used the data to pull students into groups for additional support.
- Student teams completed problem solving and were then paired with another team to compare their processing steps and answers. Students made revisions to the work as needed during the conversation.

3. PRODUCT

DEFINE:

Construct and provide different tasks and artifacts used by learners to demonstrate understanding of content. Effective products are aligned, authentic, and meaningful to learning outcomes. Giving students choices of products can increase the chances of students finding one that they believe they can do well.

RATIONALE:

Assigning one product option is likely to lead to some or many students not succeeding. Consider if the learning target is to show understanding of the laws of motion. If the only option is to write a paper that explains the laws, including examples, there may be students who have a deep knowledge of the content but struggle with their writing skills to communicate. These students might do better with alternative tasks, such as give a talk while using a poster to showcase their ideas, participate in a question and answer session with the teacher, or create a draw that illustrates the laws in everyday activities or sports, including diagrams.

If the emphasis is on demonstrating understanding of the science content, having options that align to those targeted concepts should be the focus. These examples reflect using learning preferences to craft choices. They are not assigned to students, but instead, they are presented for the learner to decide which one he or she finds appealing.

Products can also be crafted to reflect real-world interests that the students may have. Sometimes such options help engage learners into a difficult concept because the topic appeals to them. These tasks also give important context for how the abstract academic content looks like in a student's frame of reference. Consider laws of motion with sports and such activities as skateboarding and four-wheeling.

The key is that all product options will enable students to demonstrate learning at the same required level regardless of the choice made. For example, will an essay and a poster hold equal value? Answer: Only if there is depth in what goes into the poster, including presenting its reflected ideas— and that the essay does not require only surface level understanding.

LEARNER CONNECTION:

Students prefer to do work that makes sense to them and that they believe can be reasonably completed. This is accomplished by using information about students' readiness, interests, and/or learning preferences, depending on the need. Using such information helps to craft product options that the learner can adequately complete without dealing with hidden obstacles, such as requiring a shy student to present his or her ideas to the whole class, when a one-to-one conversation or writing option would be more appropriate. Having good product options helps to improve the formative assessment data received.

EXAMPLES:

- Students complete a learning menu that includes multiple options to show their understanding.
- A Think-Tac-Toe offers nine squares that include tasks that may be differentiated by readiness, interests, and/or learning preferences. Students may be tasked to complete three in a row. Another option may be to choose one task per row or column, which requires students to explore different components of a topic or concept. For example, each column may focus

on a different law of motion. Each box per column is a different level of complexity.

- Offer students three options to complete a task. The teacher designs the first two tasks. The third option challenges students to propose their own product idea that when completed will address the required skills and concepts.

Learner Voice and Access

4. READINESS

DEFINE:

Plan learning experiences at the level that is appropriate to what each student needs. Each learner is challenged to stretch his or her skills and progress in his or her growth. Students need supports that help them understand the concepts and skills from basic to complex levels. This need exists for learners who are below, at, and above the standard expectation. Readiness ensures that students work on tasks at their instructional level, with appropriate complexity. Ongoing data review of assessments drive the types of differentiation needs. This can happen through a simple practice of using exit cards to check understanding of a math concept, which leads to forming groups for the next lesson. Or use a preassessment after doing a preview of new content. Use the data to determine a start point for instruction and small group coaching.

RATIONALE:

Students engage into the curriculum experiences when the tasks look inviting to them. A message by teachers for all tasks should sound like: "You can accomplish this challenge. I have scaffolds to keep you from falling beyond any chance for success. There are opportunities that ensure that the work matches your level of understanding."

Lev Vygotsky's theory of the zone of proximal development reminds educators that learning happens when individuals are stretched just outside of their comfort zone. Set the tasks at the appropriate readiness level so that students grow into a new level of competency. This is also true for educators when it comes to deepening their skills for differentiation. Knowing one's comfort zone for teaching allows for consciously stretching oneself into new ways that seem attainable. The major growth target, such as differentiation multiple times every day, may initially appear too far to accomplish, instead take a couple of steps in the desired direction through practicing differentiation. Eventually, those small steps will pave a path that reaches the desired goal.

Readiness is a student-controlled component. While teachers develop lessons, students determine if those learning experiences are attainable. If their perception, and perception can be everything to them, is that the required tasks are too difficult or beneath their skills, they may disengage.

When factoring readiness into planning, teachers need to be accurate in matching needs to students. They also need to communicate to students how the match will benefit them. Sometimes this requires convincing learners that they can achieve "this time," because from the student's perspective of previous years of failure, they have lost confidence in themselves. Addressing readiness usually also requires mediating student's perceptions about the work, which is something explored regarding the implications of environment.

EXAMPLES:

- Place students in guided reading groups or guided math groups. Assignments to groups depend on assessment of the students' current skill levels. Students may move up or down in groups based on their academic needs.
- Provide a tiered assignment to students who are grouped by similar skill level. The task is originally devised to meet the needs of students at the targeted learning level. The task is then duplicated and revised at levels of complexity with supports and/or complexity with greater challenge based on the student groupings. All assignment formats are respectful to stretching each group of learners.
- Provide a center activity where students go to each station to complete tasks. The work may be color-coded, such as green for advanced, red for at grade level, and blue for scaffold support. Students are assigned a color, which they use for completing tasks at each center. The teacher changes up the colors with each use of the centers strategy.
- Give student groups a Think-Tac-Toe or Think Dot. There may be two or three versions based on the different group levels needed. Students are assigned the task that best serves their needs.

5. INTERESTS

DEFINE:

Instruction provides opportunities that engage students based on what interests them. Personal connections places content into a personal context that the learner finds meaningful based on what they value as important.

RATIONALE:

When students explore concepts and skills in an area that interests them, they are more likely to make connections. They may also be willing to spend more time on the tasks because the work appears engaging to them. Offering choices allow students to decide their own way. This empowerment of student voice can lead to greater buy-in of investing time.

LEARNER CONNECTION:

Students like to be in control of their lives, especially in what is typically the highly structured realm called school. Giving students choices can be motivating provided they like any of the options. Choices tend to be determined by teachers. When students' interests are incorporated, the choices become more targeted and likely to represent something that is appealing to students.

Another consideration is to include students in deciding the choices. Such experiences can promote agency skills like communication, collaboration, and taking the initiative. Give them the learning targets being practiced or assessed and then sit back as the students wrestle with the best ways to demonstrate their understanding. This approach can increase student engagement and place the heavy lifting of thought process on them.

EXAMPLES:

- Provide students with three product options to complete an assignment, such as with learning menus.
- When delivering content, craft centers where students get to choose three of four stations to gather information. One station might have a play list of three videos from which students choose one to view. Another station gives details of how experts in the field use the skills or address the focused event. A third station includes several articles, while a fourth has the same articles on recordings for listening.
- Let students choose their own writing prompt or research topic. They might also decide on the media used to express their communication, such as an article, podcast, or video. All three options would require a detailed outline to be submitted before working on their chosen option.
- Run literature circles. Students choose their novel and are grouped by like-interest as they study the literary concepts.

6. LEARNING PREFERENCES

DEFINE:

Respectful learning experiences that consider the multiple ways that each student processes content and explores and demonstrates his or her understanding. People are complex thinkers who process information in several ways.

Information provided in multiple formats such as video, lecture, and self-exploration has a greater chance of all students learning than if only one approach is used. No person does well within a single learning style, modality, or psychological framework (John Hattie).[5] The challenges with learning styles versus learning preferences are addressed in Chapter 5. It is important to expose all students to a mixture of content, process, and product options. Learning preferences is not about isolating students by thinking. It is about exposing students to diverse ways of processing concepts and skills so that what comes easily mixes with moments of cognitive dissonance. Growth happens.

LEARNER CONNECTION:

Every learner experiences moments when instruction does not make sense to them. In some cases, they find ways to make the needed connections on their own. Yet, there is just as often a sense of surface-level understanding to feeling totally in the dark. Using multiple learning preferences approaches enables teachers to plan cross-training experiences for students. This method is addressed later in the book. It ensures that students are exposed to curriculum through multiple viewpoints. Some part of this multifaceted experience will open doorways of understanding that the traditional approach cannot do for all students.

EXAMPLES:

- Use learning preferences cards to capture student learning interests and preferences. The results are used for forming tasks and center activities that stretch students through multiple perspectives.
- Students choose from RAFTs (role, audience, format, topic plus strong verb) writing prompts that are crafted, keeping in mind learning preferences. Students are not told which prompt matches what learning preferences. They simply choose what appeals to them most. This combines choice and processing preferences.[6]
- During direct instruction, the teacher incorporates different learning preferences elements for presenting and processing the content. Students are exposed to a variety of viewpoints in the material.

7. LEARNING ENVIRONMENT: CULTURE

DEFINE:

Designing the space into an area that encourages success for all learners, such as pods and circles for collaboration and spaces where individuals can reflect or small groups can have quiet conversations, or craft messages about the roles and responsibilities that determine the level of agency that students actually have over their learning experiences. How are they co-planners of their learning? Where does their voice carry weight in the learning and related conversations? To what extent is teacher control exerted over student voice versus compliance?

RATIONALE:

Learner success is dependent in part on how nurturing or sterile is the classroom culture. Like employees at an organization, students will thrive when they want to be a part of the classroom and school culture. This includes how the area is set up in rows or pods, to ready access to tools for just-in-time student needs, such as a leveled reading library, computer devices, and adult volunteers. Universal design for learning (UDL) provides a clear focus on considerations for structuring a space so that learners can succeed. Global success skills such as collaboration and communication play an important role in fostering a culture that encourages and develops students' skills to help personalize their learning.[7]

LEARNER CONNECTION:

When Sienna usually goes to math class she's filled with anxiety. The concepts do not come easy and frustration can set in quickly if she's left alone with a task for too long. This year, geometry has felt different. The teacher encourages students to ask questions. He also puts students into learning groups to bounce ideas off each other as they tackle problems and other tasks. Sienna asks questions frequently—even some that indicate that lack of confidence is more of an issue than actual skill level. The teacher patiently guides her with answers or questions, depending on what's needed at the time. He never rushes. If time is limited in that moment, he schedules a support time and follows up as promised.

Other times, Sienna gets and gives support to the other students in the various learning groups she participates in. Nine weeks into the course, Sienna is still asking questions, but not as frequently. Her confidence has grown as the teacher consistently makes himself available, is encouraging, and provides different supports through grouping students by readiness levels and interest.

EXAMPLES:

- Develop, with students' assistance, class norms for collaboration and communication. Promote agency by co-creating common language for what
each skill looks like so that students can recognize productive and constructive behavior versus actions that undermine the culture. For example:

Collaboration is being:

  - A good listener
  - Helpful to others
  - Dependable with completing tasks
  - An active contributor or participant
- Demonstrate patience with students' questions and frustrations. Students
are keen observers of behavior, especially that of the adults who appear to
be in control of their world, known as the classroom. Modeling consistent
supportive patience, even in the face of someone who does not reciprocate,
can go a long way to the student community following suit.
- Give feedback that is kind, specific, and constructive.[8] Students need to
hear what they are doing well so that they can repeat those actions. Critical
feedback can be given in the same way. Using language that is respectful
and sensitive to the student, a teacher or student can give specific feedback
that is couched in constructive language. Ron Berger, in *An Ethic of Excellence: Building a Culture of Craftsmanship with Students*, explains the
power of this feedback approach for the writing process of multiple drafts
and critiques, which can lead to quality products. Differentiation through
such feedback empowers students with personalized guidance.

8. *LEARNING ENVIRONMENT: RELATIONSHIPS*

DEFINE:

Getting to know each learner in terms of academic skills, perceptions of the
gifts and challenges they bring, and perspective of how their home life shapes
them. Build a respectful relationship of equals in terms of working together
on content instruction and achievement.

RATIONALE:

Relationships matter. In every workplace—whether it's a classroom, office,
or sports team—when individuals feel respected, supported, and empowered,
they are more likely to be productive and willing to try any task set before
them. This is especially true in classrooms where students compete for the
attention of the teacher. An instructor or principal who takes the time to

know everyone's name and something about their personal life is on a path for future success.

How Full Is Your Bucket? by Tom Rath and *Have You Filled a Bucket Today? A Guide to Daily Happiness for Kids* by Carol McCloud and David Messing are good references to the importance of relationship building for adults and children. Each uses the metaphor of positive actions filling a person's bucket or emotional bank account, while negative actions empty one's emotional bucket. Yelling and sarcasm diminishes a relationship, where students may quickly turnoff from the adult, who may be unaware of the consequences from their actions. Once a student turns off, he may no longer focus on the instruction. This concern occurs in all school settings, whether the environment is urban, rural, or suburban. The experience may look different, but the response to how language[9] is used can have a similar impact. Only extensive repairing of the relationship *might* bring around the student.

Relationships matter.

LEARNER CONNECTION:

Ten minutes into the first day of English, Antonio wants to transfer to another class. The teacher announced that the students would be required to publish writing on the course website, and worse, they would submit some of their writing for publication to newspapers and magazines at least once each semester. Antonio hates writing. He's never been good at it, and now this year, if he stays with this teacher, the whole world will know how horrible he is at writing.

On hearing Antonio's request for a pass to the counselor's office for a class change, the teacher politely asks why. Something in the teacher's manners, genuine concern, and a nonjudgmental receipt of his request, convinces Antonio to express his "hatred" for writing.

The teacher responds with one request, "Will you give me one marking period to show you that you can be a good writer? I promise that nothing you write will be posted on the classroom website or submitted to publishers without your permission."

Surprised and relieved, Antonio agreed. By the end of the first semester, he had several articles posted on the classroom website, and he was one of the first in the class to have something published in the local newspaper.

Relationships matter.

EXAMPLES:

- Get to know students by name and something about their lives.
- Use learning profile cards (see in Chapter 9) to gather information about what each student likes to do when not at school, what subjects they like, and those for which they lack confidence.

- Avoid sarcasm as a form of humor, even if some students use it. Being on the receiving end is different from dishing it out.
- Be a good listener and show supreme patience.

THE "REAL" DIFFERENTIATION RELATIONSHIP

To own learning, one must be given the power to affect their own learning. The concept "teaching and learning" is inherently codependent. Teaching is not effective if learning does not take place. Intentional learning, based on curriculum expectations, does not happen unless effective and targeted instructional experiences are provided. John Hattie uses the term "expert" teachers for those who use "diagnosis, intervention, and evaluation of their impact" (*Visible Learning and the Science of How We Learn*)[10] to self-reflect. The eight elements of differentiation are facets to the lens for meeting learner needs. Not using the differentiation lens is like aiming for a target that's obscured by a tall wall. You can lob a couple of attempts but without knowing the exact location, any connection is happenstance.

The key is to align the *instructional planning* elements—content, process, and product—with the *learner access* elements—readiness, interests, and learning preferences. All of this is done within the sphere of influence created from the environment—culture and relationships. When teachers craft learning experiences for content, processing, and products, they can find greater targeted success when considering the readiness levels, interests, and learning preferences of students. Student feedback in these areas for influencing content, processing, and products is known as student voice. This interrelationship is a core theme that is further explored in the chapters that follow.

FINAL THOUGHTS

The challenge for learning is greatest for students. At the beginning of this chapter, Mr. John's story was one that all teachers face every year. He had three preps that year, which is common at the secondary level to teach three different courses in the day with different students. Most elementary teachers in self-contained classes teach all subjects during the day but within the challenges of a schedule that is typically not of their choosing. Those elementary teachers who teach one to two subjects to different groups of students are still constrained by the challenges of the schedule as their colleagues. Teachers from all grade and age levels confront challenges in meeting learning targets for all of their students.

On the other side of the equation are the students. At the elementary level, they must tackle all subject areas. Later in their secondary career, students will have to successfully complete multiple courses and do so while navigating the different structures and approaches to instruction by—usually—an equal number of teachers. It's like working for four or more bosses who expect work products within different visions of quality.

The elements for differentiation are important lenses that collectively provide a foundation for learning. Understanding each for what they are and the purpose that they serve for the learner and learning experiences can lead to achievements by the students and their teachers.

INVITATIONS TO REFLECTION

As a result of this chapter, use the lens for differentiation to consider the following questions for a self-guided exploration of your practice and those who you support.

1. How have you seen any of the following elements in action?
   a. Instructional planning: content, process, and product
   b. Learner access: readiness, interests, and learning preferences
   Why might it be valuable for learners to experience a combination of elements in a lesson?
2. What is the educational value of paying attention to culture and relationships? What obstacles need to be overcome for environmental elements to flourish?
3. What are ways to learn several things about every student that you teach?
4. If each person learns at a different pace and starts from different levels of skills, why should we include into instructional planning a student's readiness, interests, and learning preferences?
5. When relationships are not an important factor in teaching and learning, how does everyone lose? How do such relationships get repaired?

Crossroad Planning Invitation

- Create a graphic organizer that you and your team can use for common language of the elements of differentiation. Consider using one of the online collaboration tools listed on www.SoAllCanLearn.org.

Facilitate a group or staff dialogue about the elements of differentiation. Explore the different roles of the elements for *Instructional Planning* from those who address *Learner Voice & Access*.

Enrichment Option

Evaluate a learning experience for deep use of one or more of the elements of differentiation.

NOTES

1. Comment regarding: 3 Ways to Plan for Diverse Learners: What Teachers Do http://www.edutopia.org/blog/differentiated-instruction-ways-to-plan-john-mccarthy#comment-199301.

2. The strategies listed and others are described at www.SoAllCanLearn.org. As will be discussed an effective strategy can be used through differentiation.

3. Sisyphus: http://www.mythweb.com/encyc/entries/sisyphus.html.

4. Carol Ann Tomlinson and Tonya R. Moon. *Assessment and Student Success in a Differentiated Classroom*. ASCD. 2013. Excerpt from Chapter 1: http://www.ascd.org/publications/books/108028/chapters/Differentiation@-An-Overview.aspx.

5. John Hattie and Gregory Yates. *Visible Learning and the Science of How We Learn*. Routledge. 2013.

6. RAFTs is a writing strategy that helps improve author craft and is often used as a cross-curricular writing tool. RAFTs is addressed in Chapter 7. More information can be found at www.SoAllCanLearn.org.

7. www.P21.org is a resource for professional and social skills needed by students on entering college, and entering into careers, of which some are yet to be created.

8. Ron Berger uses the terms "be kind," "be specific," and "be helpful" with regards to giving feedback in *An Ethic of Excellence: Building a Culture of Craftsmanship with Students*. Grant Wiggins described feedback as "goal-referenced; tangible and transparent; actionable; user-friendly (specific and personalized); timely; ongoing; and consistent" ("Seven Keys to Effective Feedback." *Educational Leadership* magazine. September 2012. http://www.ascd.org/publications/educational-leadership/sept12/vol70/num01/Seven-Keys-to-Effective-Feedback.aspx.) Jan Chappuis in her *Educational Leadership* article, "How Am I Doing?" (September 2012), emphasizes the need for targeted feedback that addresses needs, while recognizing strengths.

9. Ron Ritchhart. *Creating Cultures of Thinking: The 8 Forces We Must Master to Truly Transform Our Schools*. Jossey-Bass. 2015.

10. John Hattie. *Visible Learning and the Science of How We Learn*. 2011. He provides an important view of a teacher known for her instructional expertise. It's well worth looking at his findings from a 2009 study about expert teachers on pages 107–108. Ron Ritchhart and Mark Church note in their first chapter how teachers may struggle with what they "specifically want their students to do mentally" (*Making Thinking Visible: How to Promote Engagement, Understanding, and Independence for All Learners*). The alignment of teaching and learning is crucial if students who struggle and those who are advanced are to get the support they need.

Chapter 2

Differentiation CAN Be Done Well

It does seem overwhelming at first but as you pointed out, many of us already have the tools and techniques in place. If I was asked how I was differentiating my instruction, I would not be sure that I was. But as I read your examples I realize that I am already doing many of these things.

—Snookjen[1]

During a workshop on project-based learning, teachers raised questions about differentiation. It's a common question asked during the different professional learning workshops. At the mention of "differentiated instruction," the stress was palatable. These teachers were required to include in their weekly lesson plans about how they were differentiating for their students. This expectation is not unreasonable, except no one—not the teachers or administrators—seemed to have a clear understanding of what differentiated instruction looked like.

Understanding what differentiation looks like can be a challenging idea. When Dr. Susan Allan[2] was the assistant superintendent of Curriculum for Grosse Pointe Schools in Michigan, the district was a pioneer in making differentiated instruction a district-wide focus. Several of their teachers commented that good differentiation was synonymous to sound common sense instruction.

When differentiation is done well, it's integrated as part of the instructional practices as a lens for planning supports for learners. Teachers with years of expertise implementing differentiation make their practice seamless. When teachers seek to become more proficient with differentiated instruction to meet the needs of their diverse learners, they feel stressed. They may wonder how do they shed light on practices that seem abstract in concept. How do they explain their approaches in language that administrators and other stakeholders understand?

THE DOROTHY PRINCIPLE

Differentiation already exists in quality instruction. Teachers already have in their professional practice the pedagogies, strategies, and experiences to provide support for their learners. What holds back teachers is not realizing what they already know and can do.

The Dorothy Principle is based on the movie adaptation of the story, *The Wizard of Oz* (1939) by Warner Bros. Dorothy goes on a dangerous and illuminating journey to find a way back home. She makes allies and braves many trials from a cranky wizard, flying monkeys, and an even crankier wicked witch. She overcomes all obstacles only to miss her balloon trip home, the only means given to her for finding her way back to Kansas. Dorothy despairs of ever getting home when Glenda the Good, her mentor, coaches her to an important realization:

Dorothy: Oh, will you help me? Can you help me?

Glenda: You don't need to be helped any longer. You've always had the power to go back to Kansas.

Dorothy: I have?

Scarecrow: Then why didn't you tell her before?

Glenda: She wouldn't have believed me. She had to learn it for herself.

Scarecrow: What have you learned, Dorothy?

Dorothy: Well, I—I think that it, that it wasn't enough just to want to see Uncle Henry and Auntie Em—and it's that—if I ever go looking for my heart's desire again, I won't look any further than my own backyard. Because if it isn't there, I never really lost it to begin with! Is that right?

Glenda: That's all it is!

Scarecrow: But that's so easy! I should've thought of it for you.

Tin Man: I should have felt it in my heart.

But Glenda gives the most important advice: "No, she had to find it out for herself."[3]

Teachers go through a similar trial. Working with class sizes that may be too numerous to overcrowded, time that might be less than adequate or desired, top-down mandates, and other initiatives that appear to take the focus away from learner needs. Under these conditions, it is sometimes difficult to keep the priority on learners learning. In the many versions that compose these challenges, differentiation is more necessary if that goal remains providing an education so all can learn.

Like Dorothy, when teachers realize that they always had skills and tools to meet the needs of their learners, a new journey begins.

The Dorothy Principle applies to the work that teachers do with their students. Teachers have the ability and do differentiation, even those who do not realize it. Those who struggle with differentiation do not realize that they already have the capacity and skills. They may need coaching or peer learning to understand how to use differentiation as a lens on planning. Some may need additional strategies or a shift in their pedagogy. Tuning one's practices for effective teaching through differentiation begins with the recognition that the profession requires ongoing self-reflection for meeting learner needs. Very few teachers do not use differentiation. The approach may be reactive to situations in the moment. The learning results may be random in success, without targeted planning. They need guidance for intentional differentiation, which is addressed later in this chapter. Those who claim that they are not differentiating instruction are not teaching.

That last statement is a bitter truth pill to swallow, but student needs are paramount. It takes conscious effort *not* to differentiate. To paraphrase Glenda the Good, "[Teachers] wouldn't have believed me. [Teachers] had to learn it for [themselves]."

The teachers from the project-based learning workshop needed to find the answer to their dilemma themselves. Too often "the answer" was being told to them. "I keep getting different definitions for differentiation," a teacher said as several nodded in agreements. Like their students, they need support and room to explore for the meaning based on their accumulated experiences.

Having heard such responses before, the teachers were lead through a protocol to promote reflection. They read the article "3 Ways to Plan for Diverse Learners: What Teachers Do" (McCarthy),[4] and then for 15 minutes discussed and used the spider web discussion protocol.[5]

Here are some of the takeaways in the teachers' voices:

- "Differentiation does not have to be stressful."
- "Affirming to know that we are differentiating 'without knowing it' but planned differentiation is valuable too."
- "Differentiation is embedded in formative assessment."
- "Differentiation is planned and unplanned. Fluid—sometimes get caught up and forget we can be flexible."
- "One take away that I had from the discussion is that differentiation should be purposefully planned, but there needs to be the ability to differentiate in the moment."

- "All teachers possess the ability to differentiate; it is naturally occurring in your teaching."

Let's review practices to explore how differentiation occurs.

MAKING DIFFERENTIATION VISIBLE

Lesson planning is an integral part of what teachers do. Even administrators and staff developers plan for learning sessions through staff meetings and workshops. A lesson takes a learning outcome and maps activities that a teacher hopes or expects will support students learning and what they need to understand.

> **Students:** Anyone of any age who studies skills and concepts to gain higher proficiency. Students range from young children to adults.

Thoughtfully crafted lessons are a thing of beauty, until they are marred by the arrival of students;) Once learners are involved, those crafted lessons reveal stress fractures and gaps, which if not addressed appropriately, the lesson will crumble into so many useless activities. What to do?

ASSISTANCE WHEN LESSON PLANS RUN INTO STUDENTS

Moments for differentiation depend on how teachers respond to the needs of students who struggle with the lesson activities and those who show mastery of the outcomes at the start. A well-prepared teacher will anticipate the needs for scaffolds and extensions based on past experience teaching the lesson, and will include a Plan B and C.

> **Scaffolds:** Design supporting tools and activities that assist students to overcome a learning gap. Scaffolds are intended to be temporary supports that are gradually reduced as learners grow in the needed skill sets.
> **Extensions:** Provide depth and complexity that respects the growth needs of advanced learners.

Teachers find themselves making adjustments based on how their students respond. Teachers implement plans and are confronted by some portion of learners who need help understanding the presented skills and concepts, and others who find the work beneath them. Support cannot wait an hour or a day. Sometimes, response time is essential. Timely response determines long-term success and failure for the student learning of the lesson outcomes, informed by the teacher's range of support.

Assessment for Learning

Collecting data on learning progress for each student is a critical process to track growth and needs. Sometimes, educators may struggle with how to use formative assessment to support learners, even as they recognize that assessments for learning are valuable and necessary. This can happen when assessment data are not reviewed and used to address learner needs but is simply recorded before moving on to the next task. Assessment for Learning, as presented by the work of Rick Stiggins and Assessment Training Institute (ATI) (http://www.rickstiggins.com/), is a topic that will be deeply explored in Chapters 3 and 4, but one important take away is that differentiated instruction *cannot* be implemented with any effectiveness unless assessment data is used to identify what students know and do not understand.

Intuitive Differentiation

There are generally two approaches to differentiating instruction. The first is intuitive differentiation. This is the work that's done in the heat of instruction, when the lesson plans meet students. How students respond—or do not react—to the plan leads to the teacher making adjustments. Sometime the changes in a plan happen after a moment's deliberation regarding the options that are immediately available:

- A boy frowns in frustration.
- A girl's half-completed work is way off track.
- One teen finishes the work in a quarter of the time.
- Another teen lays his head on a desk.
- An adult student spends the work time playing a gem game.

The response to each situation will vary depending on the data collected as to what, why, and how (see Table 2.1):

- What is it about the activity that has led the student to his or her action?
- Why has the student chosen the response?
- How might the learning needs be addressed so that the student will resume the work?

Table 2.1. Common Interventions

Observation	What	Why	How
A boy frowns in frustration.	The directions were lengthy and rapidly delivered.	The student felt lost as to where to begin. Confused, he gave up.	Chunk the directions, rephrase in more student-friendly language, and provide in writing. Direct the student's focus on the first step. Follow up frequently to track and guide his progress.
A girl's half-completed work is way off track.	During whole group instruction, one of the steps was misunderstood, based on her work.	Having misunderstood a key step in the process, she repeats the mistake throughout the assignment.	Provide one-to-one coaching regarding the error, and then follow up with a short mini-lesson review of the step with the whole class, just in case others are making the same error.
One teen finishes the work in a quarter of the time.	The student already has the skills being taught in the lesson.	The teen knocked out the work quickly so that she could focus on more challenging work from another class.	Provide extensions that stretch her understanding of the concepts. If that's not available, let her do work from the other class while you plan something meaningful for her during the next class.
Another teen lays his head on a desk.	The task is too complex for the student.	He feels out of his depth because he lacks many of the foundational skills. Where others in his situation might disrupt the class, he chooses to be productive by taking a nap.	Provide one-to-one coaching by becoming his work partner or pairing him with a student who has good empathy skills. Either incorporate scaffolds that enable him to find success with the work, or if this is not possible, change his tasks to focus on what he needs. Be considerate of his confidence and perception of the work.
An adult student spends the work time playing a gem game.	The tasks lack clarity as to how they relate to the adult student.	This student does not understand the value of the work. Believing that the work is beneath him, he's chosen his own professional development task.	Provide one-to-one coaching support where context of the work is specifically connected to the student's professional work. Job-embedded connections are critical to all students. When such meaning is made, students are more likely to take on the tasks.

Table 2.1 shows how skilled[6] teachers manage needs during lessons. One of the means to ensure monitoring for success, obstacles, and failures of the lesson activities is observations based on a constant scan of the students in the room or online. The results are used to make adaptations to meet all students' needs.

Anytime a student asks a question, the teacher response is a potential differentiated support. Whether the teacher answers the question with a coaching question, a direct answer, an adjusted task meant to lead the student to what they need, or a promise to follow up individually, the result is that student received the help required.

CROSSROAD LESSONS

Differentiation can be most effective by planning ahead of time for when those opportunities present themselves. Anticipating students' needs is like having the gift of accurately predicting the future. Seeing the actual outcome can be a hazy proposition. At a minimum, any teacher can make predictions of the common areas of needs in a lesson based on previous experiences teaching the objectives. Such basic predictions can bring an outcome more in focus for meeting student needs.

Try this reflection challenge. Think about an upcoming lesson, or past lesson, that was important in the learners' growth. When previously taught, recall the faces of some of the students who struggled or were so overwhelmed that they shut down, such as by resting their head in their arms. Consider the data from formative assessments from that experience, especially for the struggling learners and those who needed more complexity.

- How might a teacher respond to support that student's growth?
- How could they be helped to move past shutting down toward rejoining the learning journey?

In these instances, teachers make adjustments, provide alternatives, and coach-up the students. Whatever it takes to help the students get back into the game, teachers find ways for success.

"Crossroad lessons" is a term to frame learning experiences that address key learning concepts that students must know. But some students will struggle. Such lessons are found throughout units of instruction and the curriculum as a whole. Knowing they exist is half the solution. The other half is collecting the just-in-time interventions used in the middle of instruction and placing them into action plans for the next time the same lesson is taught.

The names of the students will change, but the needs for those who struggle and others who need more challenge will remain. Having planned supports and interventions ready to use, prior to teaching the lesson, anticipates learner needs with prepared resources. Save time by attending to needs before frustration reaches a negative level where students lose faith in their ability, and they give up.

As seen in Table 2.1, common interventions, crossroad lessons are also opportunities to meet the needs of advance learners before boredom reaches a level of devaluing the content. Once that happens, these students will disconnect from the course, giving just enough effort to minimally attain what they think is needed, while focusing their energies on more important needs from other courses and personal hobbies. Plan for learning tasks that stretch their growth. The work should be respectful to what they need and not tasks to keep them busy, such as tutoring or extra work. These learners need to stretch their thinking. The result is students pushing the envelope of what they are capable of doing, and becoming stronger scholars from the experiences.

Here are some examples of learning experiences that evolved from the student needs that reoccurred every year on improving writing details and use of word choice.

Portrait Writing

Through writing, students paint a picture of a location like the trophy case. They must include the five senses of sight, sound, smell, taste, and touch. For taste, there is no "tasting" the wall or other objects. Students take smells and turn them into taste descriptions. For an extra challenge for some students, ban all sight-based words.

Detail Riddles

Take students outside or into the cafeteria immediately after lunch. Each student looks for three to four objects such as a juice bottle, an aluminum foil wrapper, or a tire of a parked car. For each item, the student collects adjectives and phrases that describe the chosen objects. They construct riddles where the object is described without naming it.

Intentional Differentiation

Changes to lessons in the moment are an integral part of practice. There are formal structures that can be used as part of planning that help improve opportunities for student achievement of learning outcomes. The Dorothy Principle that teachers already know how to differentiate is based on their active use of intuitive differentiation. The challenge is for teaching to be about working more efficiently and having students tackling the heavy lifting of learning.

Intentional differentiation is the planning that occurs prior to instruction based on assessment data. Reflecting on and implementing the elements of differentiation into lessons provides strategic support of student learning. Being intentional depends on how much is known about the students in the areas of academics (readiness), interests, and their sense making (learning preferences). Each of these student perspectives is explored throughout this book. What is important to understand now is that the more that is known about students within these areas, the more teachers can do to improve differentiating lessons to meet the needs of all learners.

Three-Dimensional Instruction

Anticipating the needs of learners in crossroad lessons is a way to make instructional planning more efficient. Considering all the work that goes into preparing lessons to engage and raise achievement of learning outcomes, having a variety of supports within the instructional structure helps.

In the book, *Classroom Instruction That Works* by Dean, Hubbell, Pitler, and Stone,[7] homework is addressed in Chapter 7. The authors found that the research literature about the effectiveness of homework had mixed results. One positive trend was that homework could be effective if purposeful. For example, the focus of homework should be on quality of work, not the amount of practice time. Using the differentiation lens, this would mean giving students different sets of tasks based on their current level of understanding. The chapter goes on to suggest that through technology, "tools not only give students 'anytime, anyplace' access but also provide them with multiple avenues to learn a concept."[8] Through differentiation, teachers should provide a variety of ways to practice skills and concepts, which might be a multistep approach that students follow. Another option is to provide different tasks and let students choose the method that best appeals to their preferences.

Both avenues can be addressed through a planning process introduced here as three-dimensional instruction. This form of intentional differentiation is a process where, in the course of a lesson, students explore the learning outcomes from at least three different perspectives. Students are meant to experience many or all of the different approaches, unless the lesson is structured to allow the student to choice of options.

Three-dimensional instruction is successful through preplanning and is recommended for supporting crossroad lessons. There are different levels of implementing this process, depending on the teacher's comfort level.

Quick Start

Plan three experiences during a lesson that includes an audio approach such as a lecture or discussion, a visual such as a video or graphic organizer, and a kinesthetic such as a reflective journal write or a physical movement like drawing letters or numbers in sand or shaving cream.

Intermediate Start

Try a more structured approach by applying the principles of learning preferences, such as Robert Sternberg's triarchic theory of multiple intelligences.[9] This approach to learning considers three different ways that learners can process information: analytical, practical, and creative. It is important to note that the theory posits that everyone can become strong in all three areas. A deeper look is taken in Chapters 6 and 9 regarding learning preferences.

Teach a lesson that incorporates three activities such as one that is analytical, the next is practical, and the final practices creativity or innovation such as genius hour.[10] Or, provide three different tasks that use each of these preferences and let students decide which one they want to complete. Students will sometimes choose a task because it interests them more than the others, or they may choose the option that appeals to them for the preference—at that moment in time.

Here's an example that can be developed following either the quick or intermediate start approach.

Learning Outcome: Identify strong voice as a writing craft tool.
Assessment: Exit Card
1. State the posted learning targets and assessment
2. Demonstrate in a selection of video clips
3. *Process*: explain to a partner what you noticed
4. Review the 6 + 1 traits rubric for voice
5. In teams of two to three, make a Frayer Model for Voice to be put on the word wall.
6. *Process*: explain to a partner the three elements for voice: word choice, details, and sentence fluency.
7. Think Dot: voice through six examples.
8. *Process*: jigsaw group members into dot teams for each of the six dots. Share solutions in Dot groups.

9. Assessment: Exit Card highlights words and phrases that enhance voice in a writing sample. Explain what the voice reflects or reminds them of, based on the words highlighted.

Power Three-Dimensional Start

This formal process is the most productive of the three. It was developed and refined through work with teachers across the United States. The quick start and intermediate start are building blocks that scaffold a teacher's journey to implementing intentional differentiation. When designing three-dimensional experiences, the more innovative ideas, especially those "way-out" imaginations, the more interesting experiences are developed that engage students toward making connections.

The planning process is made of five simple steps.

1. **Identify the learning outcome(s)**

    Start with an active verb from the domains of knowledge. "I can" statements are another thought starter that can incorporate these ideas.

2. **List and decide on the best formative assessment(s)**

    This product or performance demonstrates the learning outcome(s). Keeping the end in mind helps ensure that the chosen activities project a learning path for students to practice skills and concepts with fidelity. Activities should be purposeful to the learning outcome(s).

3. **Brainstorm 9 to 21 different ways to teach the concepts and skills of the learning outcome(s) (12 or more is best)**

    Think outside of the box for ideas. Record mostly concrete and practical applications over abstract activities. A variety of ideas open opportunities for rich experiences that support learners who struggle with traditional approaches and stretch advanced students in having deeper learning experiences.

4. **Build the lesson steps**

    Include three or more ideas from the brainstorm list. Half of the list may get scrapped as not appropriate to the focus or just brainstorm crud. That leaves 6–11 useful ideas to be included in 2–3 lessons. Using at least three ideas in a lesson provides multiple ways to engage students with making sense of the concepts.

    Where a typical lesson traditionally provides experiences mostly in one perspective, three-dimensional instruction offers at least two more points of view. As will be explored in a later chapter, students need moments to process new content before adding more to their plate of understanding. Through reflection, students can digest an instructional activity before more components are added.

5. Develop needs for scaffolds and extensions

A predictable outcome of assessments is that some students will likely not succeed and others may likely exceed course- or grade-level expectations. Using the ideas of intentional differentiation, discussed earlier in this chapter, teachers can anticipate the supports needed by students who underachieve on assessments to help them develop the targeted concepts and skills. They also plan extensions so that the high achievers can stretch and grow in their learning.

Example Lesson Based on Three-Dimensional Approach

Lesson Differentiation Reflection Guide—Template

Grade:
Subject(s):

Step One: Identify the learning outcomes
Concepts:

Knowledge/Facts:

Skills:

Step Two: List and decide on the best formative assessments
Lead to the learning outcome(s)
Examples: exit tickets, quiz, observational checklist, performance, student feedback

Step Three: Brainstorm 9–21 different ways to teach the concepts and skills

Step Four: Build the lesson steps
Outline the differentiated lesson using 3+ differentiated experiences from Step Three.
Include at least:
1 Content &/or product experience
2+ Processing experiences

Step Five: Develop needs for scaffolds and extensions
A) For learners who are NOT successful for this lesson (see steps 1 and 2), what scaffolds will you plan to help them get what they need?

B) For learners who exceed lesson expectations (see steps 1 and 2), what extensions will you plan to ensure their continued growth?

Figure 2.1. Lesson Differentiation Reflection Guide—Template

Lesson Differentiation Reflection Guide — Example One

Grade: 7—9
Subject(s): English — Writing

Step One: Identify the learning outcomes
Concepts:
Details build understanding that readers can follow for a variety of purposes and genres.

Knowledge/Facts:
Types of details — facts, illustrations, examples, and sensory
Usage focus: Fiction, Non-fiction, persuade, informational, and explain

Skills:
Crafting writing using a variety of details formats.

Step Two: List and decide on the best formative assessments
Lead to the learning outcome(s)
Examples: exit tickets, quiz, observational checklist, performance, student feedback
    A. Think-Pair-Share for feedback and revision
    B. Inference-based Riddles — Chosen option
    C. Graphic organizer of details
    D. Journal reflections: written or video recorded

Step Three: Brainstorm 9–21 different ways to teach the concepts and skills
1. Fastwrite
2. Fastwrite — Freewrite Strategy
3. Window Activity
4. Author's Craft: deconstruct articles and passages
5. Graphic Organizer on using the 5 senses to describe Person, Place, and Ideas
6. Story Plot Tree analogy by John Jakes
7. RAFTs: Choosing details based on the audience
8. Portrait writing strategy
9. Craft Inference Riddles
10. Taste Test descriptors
11. Presentation on different forms of details
12. Explore different forms of details, ex. Illustrations, quotes, facts, sensory, and examples
13. Giving and Following Directions activity
14. Story Tag Team Relay
15. Brainstorm descriptors (individually and/or teams)
16. Explore Word Choice via 6+1 Writing Traits
17. Drawing Mini-Lesson
18. Monster Drawing Replication activity
19. Reading Protocols that share passages, ex. Save the last Word for Me, Say Something, and Harkness/Spider Discussion
20. Chalk Talk protocol
21. Outlining strategies: storyboards, webs, and graphic organizers
22. Feedback and Revision on writing
23. Podcasting using a script or talking points outline
24. Gallery Walk protocol

Figure 2.1. Continued

Step Four: Build the lesson steps
Outline the Differentiated Lesson using 3+ differentiated experiences from Step Three.
Include at least:
1 Content &/or Product experience
2+ Processing experiences

1. Lesson Launch: *Giving and Following Directions activity*
   Students give directions for how to tie shoelaces or make a sandwich, while the teacher tries to complete the task. Where directions are vague or lack specificity, the teacher does something different. Use this experience to illustrate the need for clear details and the need for a variety of detail formats.
2. State the Learning Outcomes
3. Direct Instruction: Teacher reviews *Word Choice from 6+1 Writing Traits* through use of 5 sensory descriptors: sight, sound, smell, taste, and touch. Use author's text to analyze examples. Use images and items, such as fruits and flowers, to support connections of the senses. Option: Include 2–3 texts at different reading levels and assign according to *homogenous groups based on reading skills.*
4. Students talk in groups of 2 or 3 regarding their understanding of Word Choice and Sensory Details
5. Teacher models an Inference Riddle
6. Students give *feedback for revision* suggestions to improve the riddle. Use as a processing activity by having students make revision suggestions in groups of 2–4, as time permits.
7. *Field Trip*: Take students into the hall, cafeteria, or outside to collect data on 2–3 items they find. These details will be used to craft the *Inference Riddle*. Use a graphic organizer for students who need it.
8. Students craft an *Inference Riddle*, either individually or in pairs.
9. Students share riddles in pairs and receive feedback in the form of 1–2 "I like..." and one "I wonder..." A *handout on types of details* is used as a guide for discussion.
10. Students make revisions.
11. Have 3–4 students share their riddles to the whole class to guess.
12. Collect all riddles. Consider posting all of them on a classroom website or other online publication.
13. Journal Reflection (video recording): What types of details did you use to create your Inference Riddle? What made it easy or difficult for others to guess?

Step Five: Develop Needs for Scaffolds and Extensions

C) For learners who are NOT successful for this lesson (see steps 1 and 2), what scaffolds will you plan to help them get what they need?
   Option 1: Provide a word bank of descriptors based on the five senses. Students with limited vocabulary or background experiences can use the list to craft their writing.
   Option 2: Review more examples of author texts. Choose writers who students are familiar with or who write about topics that interest them.
   Option 3: Use the Window Activity as a follow up writing experience.

D) For learners who EXCEED lesson expectations (see steps 1 and 2), what extensions will you plan to ensure their continued growth?
   Option 1: Have students practice crafting fewer "Sight" descriptors and more "Taste" and "Smell" descriptors. Taste can be very challenging to write when describing objects like a soda bottle, car tire, or trophy case.

Figure 2.1. Continued

Option 2: Review more examples of author texts that tend to be more complex in their writing skills. Have students deconstruct authors' use of word choice for different purposes and genres, and evaluate their success.
Option 3: Use the Window Activity to deepen the students' perspective as they write from different points of view.

Figure 2.1. Continued

FINAL THOUGHTS

The skills for differentiated instruction are already within what teachers know how to do. Effective teachers collect formative data during the lessons. They provide in-the-moment support based on students' response to the learning experiences. This is the basis of intuitive differentiation.

Flexibility in the heat of the moment is a gift that effective teachers use on a daily basis. Through experience, they identify the reoccurring crossroad lessons that need scaffolds and extensions for the future students they teach. The challenges of crossroad lessons tend to reoccur even as the students change. Even so, the wise educator knows to remain alert. No matter the lesson revisions to anticipate reoccurring needs, there will always be students who bring forth a new need to be tackled in the moment.

Effective learning experiences include intuitive and intentional differentiation. Both coexist in teaching and learning. Preplanned or intentional differentiation uses structures, such as three-dimensional instruction and formative assessments, to alter future lessons based on the needs of all learners.

It's hard to support students' growth without specific data that inform on what they know and do not know. Armed with actionable data, teachers can plan lessons that strategically address needs just as a surgeon prepares for an operation by reviewing the patient's vital information. Operating on a patient, as with teaching students, after ignoring or not looking at relevant data is at best a guarantee for frustration, at worst it's malpractice. Formative assessment informs intuitive and intentional differentiated instruction to ensure a healthy and successful learner.

INVITATIONS TO REFLECTION

As a result of this chapter, use the lens for differentiation to consider the following questions for a self-guided exploration of your practice and those whom you support.

1. What are ways that you differentiate in your practice that might be invisible to the non-educator's eye? How can that practice be explained for parents, school board members, or other stakeholders to understand?

2. What are the ways to raise the level of intuitive differentiation in your practice by anticipating needs?
3. What crossroad lessons could you preplan with intentional differentiated strategies based on formative assessments?
4. Consider how you might design a lesson following a three-dimensional instructional approach: quick start, intermediate start, and/or power start.
5. Review a crossroad lesson for use of intuitive and intentional differentiation. How might you expand the intentional differentiation? How will this change the anticipation focus of the intuitive differentiation?

Crossroad Planning Invitation

• Intentional differentiations: Design or revise a learning experience for an upcoming concept that learners in the past have struggled with.
• Facilitate a group or staff discussion on examples of intuitive and intentional differentiation. Discuss the value of planning Crossroad learning experiences.

Enrichment Option

Design a learning experience that uses the Power three-dimensional approach.

NOTES

1. Quote comes from a teacher who was commenting on the article: "3 Ways to Plan for Diverse Learners: What Teachers Do." August 28, 2015. http://www.edutopia.org/blog/differentiated-instruction-ways-to-plan-john-mccarthy#comment-194791.

2. Susan Allan and Carol Tomlinson. *Leadership for Differentiating Schools and Classrooms.* ASCD, Alexandria, VA. 2000.

3. Movie Quote DB: http://www.moviequotedb.com/movies/wizard-of-oz-the/quote_26339.html.

4. John McCarthy. "3 Ways to Plan for Diverse Learners: What Teachers Do," Edutopia: July 23, 2014. http://www.edutopia.org/blog/differentiated-instruction-ways-to-plan-john-mccarthy.

5. Dayna Laur. "Spider Web Discussions as a Formative Assessment." December 14, 2014. http://daynalaur.com/assessment/spider-web-discussions-formative-assessment/. This protocol is similar to the Harkness Discussion protocol.

6. The teacher response by anticipation and preparation ahead of the lesson are some of the attributes that John Hattie references for expert teachers in visible learning and the *Science of How We Learn* (2011), pages 107–108. Well worth reading and reflecting as they are attributes for intentional differentiation, which is explored in the next section.

7. Ceri B. Dean, Elizabeth Ross Hubbell, Howard Pitler, and Bj Stone. *Classroom Instruction That Works: Research-Based Strategies for Increasing Student Achievement*, 2nd Edition. ASCD, Alexandria, VA. 2013.

8. Chapter Seven: *Assigning Homework and Providing Practice* (Kindle location 1915)

9. Robert Sternberg's triarchic theory of multiple intelligences:

"What Does It Mean to Be Smart?" *Educational Leadership*. March 1997. http://www.ascd.org/publications/educational-leadership/mar97/vol54/num06/What-Does-It-Mean-to-Be-Smart%C2%A2.aspx.

"Recognizing Neglected Strengths." *Educational Leadership*. September 2006. http://www.ascd.org/publications/educational-leadership/sept06/vol64/num01/Recognizing-Neglected-Strengths.aspx.

"Allowing for Thinking Styles." *Educational Leadership*. November 1994. http://www.ascd.org/publications/educational-leadership/nov94/vol52/num03/Allowing-for-Thinking-Styles.aspx.

10. Genius hour: This is a constructivist approach that strongly encourages student voice in their learning. A deeper look is taken in the chapter on natural structures for differentiation.

Chapter 3

Assessments Matter: Making Learning Specific and Realistic

> Differentiation is making sure that the right students get the right learning tasks at the right time. Once you have a sense of what each student holds as "given" or "known" and what he or she needs in order to learn, differentiation is no longer an option; it is an obvious response.
>
> —Lorna M. Earl[1]

What if a skilled pitcher was given the important job of throwing a ball to hit a target? Every time he or she hits the target, the result would benefit a group of people by bettering their lives. Each time he or she missed, those same people would find their lives more difficult. And if he or she missed repeatedly, the likelihood of turning around the people's circumstances may become irreversible.

Shouldering this pressure, the pitcher receives news that is a mix of benefits and challenges. The beneficial news is that the target is large, the size of a barn door. On being hit, it makes a bell sound like crystals clinking and glows for two seconds. The challenges are that the room is absolutely dark, the door moves vertically, laterally, away, close-up, and occasionally teleports to a different part of the room.

In education, teachers face a similar challenge every day. Those who are trained in unpacking standards and curriculum guides have learning targets that their students must accomplish. Without differentiation, success is fleeting and often a lucky hit. Students who struggle will continue to, if their specific needs are not met. Advanced learners who are school savvy find success mostly regardless of what approaches the teacher takes. The result is that struggling students may become more frustrated and give up on themselves and the teachers who struggle to help. Advanced learners may meet expectations of the standards and curriculum guide, but they miss the experiences of deepening their understanding of the complexities and moving ahead with curriculum as needed.

Differentiation is the lens that provides a clear view of the paths that supports academic success. The differentiation lens encourages teachers to use snapshots of each pupil to create learning experiences so that students can learn at the pace and depth that they need. But simply differentiating through intuitive approaches will create only slight improvements. It would be like the pitcher eyeing the throwing target, while wearing glasses of the wrong prescription. For differentiation to effectively put the target into focus and reveal the door's movement patterns, full commitment in using assessments is required. Differentiation and assessments make an unbeatable combination for learner achievements.

Assessments focus differentiated support on learners. Having common language regarding assessments is important to this conversation and the impact on differentiation. Assessment in general has been defined in many ways. The Assessment Reform Group (2002)[2] provides one that will be used for this chapter:

> Assessment for learning is the process of seeking and interpreting evidence for use by learners and their teachers to decide where the learners are in their learning, where they need to go and how best to get there.

ASSESSMENT FOR LEARNING

Rick Stiggins, during a presentation in Southeast Michigan in the first decade of 2000, compared summative and formative assessments in a way that resonates today. Summative assessments are like autopsies. The job of the coroner is to evaluate the body to find the cause of death. Once he or she completes this task, he or she moves on to the next body. A summative assessment provides information on what students have accomplished and where their lack of skills still exists on a topic. The results are little used afterward as teachers move forward with the curriculum. For example, semester exams and state standardized tests often represent this result.

Formative assessments are like seeing one's family physician during a routine health checkup. If the doctor notices something that concerns him or her, he or she may have the patient take some tests or follow a protocol at home. Later in the following week, there may be another visit for the doctor to track progress, make a diagnosis, and determine if further work needs to be done.

Assessment for learning is about using data for the purpose of meeting students where they are with what they need. There is no one size fits all for learning, yet the prevailing teacher practice continues this route. A means to empower teachers to become more targeted in their support is to use a formative assessment cycle.

FORMATIVE ASSESSMENT CYCLE

Formative assessment cycle (FAC) is about meeting the needs of all students by collecting data on what they know and do not know. Often, teachers do assessments that get this information, record the data, and move on to the next task or lesson. The result is not formative assessment, but summative. Summative assessments record student status for meeting key objectives and then moving on to a new focus. For every summative assessment, a teacher should consider doing 5–10 formative assessments.

Effective FAC basics include the following steps:

1. Collect data from a learning experience.
2. Analyze the data for what students know and do not know.
3. Reflect on the data to plan interventions and/or extensions and enrichments.
4. Implement plan of action.
5. Repeat Steps 1–4.

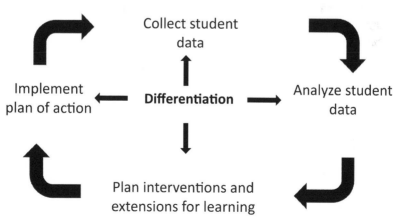

Figure 3.1. **Formative Assessment Cycle for Differentiation**

1. Collect Data from a Learning Experience

Teachers provide learning experiences for the purpose of helping students meet specific learning targets. Each lesson has a specific outcome that students should be able to demonstrate, whether it's a basic skill that requires 40–60 minutes, or a complex concept that may be addressed over a series of "building block" activities across several days. Tracking students' progress daily is critical for ensuring that they do not fall behind without being noticed. The last thing anyone wants is to spend days or weeks on a unit and discover only with the summative assessment that students were stuck early on.

Use a variety of assessment strategies to gather data on student learning from each lesson, such as Exit Cards, KWL charts, need-to-know charts, and gallery walks. Ensure that the method used targets the heart of the skill(s) and/or concept(s) that students should acquire. The following example shows the complete cycle. Step 1 reflects the purpose of this section:

Exit Cards (Sometimes Called Ticket Out the Door)

This is a quick strategy that some schools use as a daily assessment tool.

1. Given five minutes at the end of a lesson, students answer one to three questions based on the learning target. Index cards or half a sheet of paper is all that's needed.
2. On collecting the cards, the teacher reviews them for learning target accuracy.
3. Consider making three piles, like a golf score:
   1s: Cards demonstrate strong knowledge of the learning target.
   2s: Cards demonstrate partial knowledge, with minor gaps.
   3s: Cards demonstrate lack of understanding, with major gaps.
4. Teacher reviews cards for trends and grouping needed to reteach or incorporate skills and/or concepts into the next lesson.
5. Teacher creates a plan of action based on the cards.
   Cards may be discarded once a plan is in place. Remember, it's a quick assessment to determine what adjustments are needed based on who and how many students did not successfully gain the expected learning outcomes.

2. Analyze the Data for What Students Know and Do Not Know

Formative assessments, which look at the data for purposes of providing support, enable teachers to think about the students' demonstrated work in terms of what parts represent the learning target, and what kinds of errors exist that are a barrier to progress. A score of 50 percent or 85 percent gives next to no information about what a student knows and does not know about a topic. This is one important reason for not grading formative assessments. Grading loses its purpose, which is to inform students and the teacher what are the learning needs.

In the Exit Card example, Steps 2–4 are key actions for unpacking and diagnosing the root of learning disconnects. Assessment data is often analyzed by looking collectively at the scores by all of the students. Sometimes, sampling is used to check on a few student results. These strategies can be useful, but they can miss important information at the individual level.

Once students are identified by their degree of understanding or not understanding a concept (Steps 2 and 3 from Exit Card example), it's important to take an individualized evaluation for the cause of student learning gaps. In the following math example, consider the assessment result by two different students' work on two-digit multiplication. One student would be rated as a 2 and the other a 3 from Step 3 of the Exit Card example. What clues from their work identify the students' needs?

Both students lack understanding of aligning the second row to being with the tens column. Student B may also struggle with multiplication. Consider how their needs might be addressed in a small group regarding alignment, and individually with Student B on multiplication. Diagnosing the possible reasons for a student's learning gaps makes reteaching and coaching targeted and time efficient.

Two-digit multiplication

Student A

24
X32
48
72
120

Student B

24
X32
46
57
103

3. Reflect on the Data to Plan Interventions and/or Extensions and Enrichments

Once student(s) needs are determined, a plan of action can be developed (Steps 4–5 from the Exit Card example). As we saw with the math example, the diagnosis is specific and requires differentiation. Alignment may have been a trend among several students, which could be addressed as a small group mini lesson or a whole class review at the beginning of the next lesson.

The multiplication skills issue may not be a common need or be addressed effectively as a whole class review. Let's not forget the students who are way past two-digit multiplication. What do we do for them to ensure they are growing? The lesson activities will need to be differentiated, and the formative assessment results will help to ensure that the coached learning experiences are targeted to what groups and individuals need.

4. Implement Plan of Action

This step in the FAC starts the process again. On implementing the plan via lessons and coaching, new formative assessment activities will need to occur to track if the students who were falling behind are back on track, or need more supports framed in different ways. It's also an opportunity to see if other students ran into stumbling blocks, or are clearly ahead of the pack, thus needing more complex work that challenges them.

FINDING TIME

Some might raise the concern about time expenditures to follow an FAC when there are pressures to forge ahead with curriculum demands. Such demands and an FAC are not at odds. Using daily quick assessment strategies like Exit Cards or nongraded quizzes gives important feedback about the success of a lesson. Which teacher or administrator exists who would prefer to be blind to whether or not students are successfully learning based on the lesson implementation?

Or another way to put it, if an educator's job is to ensure that all students are learning, then tracking success and gaps is essential. Reteaching blindly wastes time both for students and teachers. An FAC helps ensure that no child falls between the cracks, much less falling behind. Per Lorna M. Earl, quoted at the opening of this chapter, it's an obvious response to facilitate successful learning for all.

Flexible and Targeted Assessments

Every teacher is confronted by the challenge and opportunity of working with groups of students whose skill levels are different. While there will be similarities or crossovers of like skills, there will also be distinct differences in what one group of students knows and understands that others do not. When a teacher delivers instruction, there will likely be some students who "get it" intuitively and others who "figure it out" after some adjustments to their thinking. But there may be some who "don't get it" intuitively nor can they on their own find the adjustments to make to "figure it out."

Teaching is being a constant learner who gets how some students think and operate. The FAC helps them to adjust their thinking about how instruction could be delivered by understanding the students' obstacles. Students of all ages and life experiences need their teacher to learn about their readiness levels of curriculum understanding and make the needed adjustments so that all can learn. Provide a variety of experiences where students work within a continuum of work that is respectful to their readiness level in that moment.

In a previous chapter, the concept of intentional planning was explored. Preplanning is critical for struggling and advanced learners. A veteran of a course or curriculum can anticipate the key learning points where there may likely be students who will need scaffolds and others who will need stretching, before they have a student roster. Prepare these learning experiences so that when the assessment data target students, adaptations can be made with time efficiency and learner needs in mind. What follows are approaches for appropriate and targeted differentiation through effective use of assessments.

Tiered Instruction

Tiered instruction[3] is an effective means of addressing student readiness needs. Guided reading exemplifies this approach. Reading comprehension data informs teachers of the current reading level of their students. Based on the data, students are placed into leveled groups, because they have similar needs. As students progress, they can be moved to the next reading level group when they need higher-level complexity. At the same time, students who find themselves falling behind in their current cohort may be moved to a group that can address their needs at an appropriate pace.

Tiering happens in all subject areas. An important practice is to keep groups fluid and flexible. Students move to where their needs can be supported. This sometimes requires teachers to leave their ego at the door. It's okay to acknowledge that they cannot adequately meet a student's needs on their own. Actively getting help from colleagues to coach them and/or directly teach the student sends the message that learners come first.

Other approaches to readiness can be done in combination with interests and learning preferences through learning centers or stations. Combine assessment data with an understanding of students' interests and ways of thinking. Students are assigned specific tasks to complete at each center that are aligned to their needs. Allow students to choose which tasks they will accomplish, such as three of four or four of six. Empowering choice allows students to pick the tasks that interest them most. Incorporating different ways to process information encourages students to choose an approach that resonates to them the most. When done, always allow students to choose their course of action, while avoiding assigning work based on learning preferences.

Support Early to Save Time Later

Students who struggle with skills and concepts do not need "easier" work. They need those basics while tackling complex ideas. The teacher has two challenges for these students: help them develop and strengthen the base skills that may be missing, and provide them with ways to tackle the learning concepts alongside other students. Basic skills can be addressed through tiered instruction where they are grouped with others who share common needs. Access to the more complex work that is grade- or course-level appropriate requires a temporary crutch.

When someone has a broken or sprained leg and the food is down a long hallway, at the bottom of a long staircase, and in the second room, we do not tell him find your way or starve, nor do we give him bread and water as basic fare until he can join everyone else. A wheelchair is provided so that he can join the others. As his strength grows, he's provided with a walker or crutches, with an aide walking along until he no longer needs that person at his side. Eventually, he walks to have meals with his own power.

Struggling students need the same meal of engaging and complex work. Provide them with the scaffolds that allow them to work with classmates at as close to the same level as possible. For example:

- Struggling readers may need a recorded version to listen to as they follow along with the passages. Or provide them with reading material that is at their comprehension level. As a result, they can engage in critique and analysis of literature, social commentary, or scientific theories.
- Provide variously completed outlines or lecture notes for students to fill in the missing parts. Now students can delve into the key ideas and how they relate to current events or important issues reflected by the subject area.
- Allow the use of calculators when the focus is not on basic computational skills so that the struggling student can get the needed data for analysis.
- Provide identified quality references for students to focus on research of content, and later address the research skills for distinguishing credible sources. Students can now decide on how best to construct their persuasive essays with a strong counterargument.

Stretch Advanced Learners until They Sweat

There is a student population that achieves high scores but learns little. One educator-parent shared how her daughter sweated through school to earn high marks. When she got to university, the work continued to be challenging, yet she had the success skills to tackle obstacles and persevere until she learned and achieved. The story is not just about how her preparation in high school prepared her for university. Students came to her for help because of her success. They did not know how to handle the academic challenges of college because they earned high grades in high school with ease. Work never consistently stretched them until they ran into the wall in college and had little experience for how to get over.

For students who are gifted or advanced in a particular skill set, launch them into deep water when the mainstream is too shallow for them. Use assessments to track what they know so that their work is attuned to their skill set. Preassessments are a common practice to know ahead of a unit or lesson what knowledge and skills students have. Done prior to the learning activity gives teachers time to plan tiered assignments with an advanced component, or work that is completely different due to the complexity of the concepts.

There is no reason to have students complete work that they already have mastered to a sufficient level. The experience and feelings can be the same when a teacher is required to attend a professional growth session about a topic that they are already quite knowledgeable.[4]

One challenge to preassessments is that once instruction begins, it becomes apparent that even more students may need more stretch then originally determined. Sometimes a preassessment is best done after students preview the concepts and skills. More students may recall levels of understanding that they had forgotten. The result may be more students who demonstrate a deeper understanding of parts or all of the learning outcomes.

Assessment checks throughout a multipart lesson, unit, or experience help to monitor how student progress ebbs and flows. This ensures that a teacher notes when students need to be stretched. Because this can happen at any time, intentional differentiation planning becomes more important to successfully ensure that needs are met for all learners.

MULTIPLE WAYS TO DEMONSTRATE LEARNING

In a fifth grade social studies class, students studied Frank Lloyd Wright's architecture. A mother sought advice about how to get her son to do the work. He had no desire to create a replica in a shoebox. Rather than force his compliance, she wanted to ignite a desire in him to want to complete the task.

Through the conversation, it became clear that her son loved to play Minecraft, a computer game where students explore and build structures in various biomes. The open sandbox framework allows for unstructured play in survival mode and creative mode. The creative option eliminates all game-based conflicts like monsters and limited resources. Players can create anything with access to all resources, for such constructs as a Frank Lloyd Wright house. The fifth grade student was excited to jump into the research and design. His teacher supported him because the end product matched what was being assessed.

Allowing differentiated products for students to demonstrate their understanding of content is an important way to motivate and better ensure that outcomes are addressed. Traditional assessments have their place in collecting data for the FAC. Using the differentiation lens for assessments gives students different ways to show what they know and provides them with better opportunities to demonstrate success. Providing traditional and alternative ways to assess learning can be effective if the outcomes are consistent regardless of the tool.

For example, if the learning target is understanding the implications of the laws of motion or the pros and cons of the United Nations, students can express themselves through a variety of ways: essay writing, presentation, artistic representations with captions or recorded details, video conference discussion with scientists or politicians, or a scripted video. While a multiple choice test might seem the easiest and convenient for teachers to collect data, it may not be the way that motivates and enables students to show their depth of knowledge.

Student voice is an important consideration as it is the lens through which students consider participation in learning experiences based on the differentiation elements: readiness, interests, and learning preferences. "We don't know what we don't know" should be a guiding principle for teachers, just as it is for students. All teachers, including those who are at the top of the profession, are limited by their perspective and experiences, which can be vast, but not encompassing everything. Students come to school with their own experiences that can bring perspective to their work. When only one type of assessment is used, sometimes this can lead to unforeseen obstacles for determining what students know and do not know.

Here are two approaches to differentiating products for assessment:

Approach One

Design two to three forms for how students can complete the work, thus giving students options. Each option respectfully addresses the learning targets clearly and at the expected level of quality. Students get to choose which task they prefer to accomplish. Having options can encourage students to choose the one that they would prefer to do.

But what if a student does not like any of the options?

Approach Two

This level of assessment includes the first approach and extends responsibility into the hands of the learner. In addition to the teacher-developed options, students are offered the chance to create their own assessment. For example, use Minecraft to design and explain Frank Lloyd Wright's architecture. The student proposal must address the learning outcomes at the expected quality level. The student does the heavy lifting of designing and proposing options. The teacher either accepts the design, negotiates revisions, or sends the student away to come up with something more appropriate as an assessment. Give students a time limit for coming up with an acceptable proposal. If time runs out, the student must choose from one of the original options presented by the teacher.

The key to the second approach is for teachers to not feel like they have to know the tools from the student's proposal, nor the logistics around delivery. In the Minecraft example, the teacher only needed to recognize how the final product could demonstrate the essential understandings from his or her curriculum and that the work could be managed within the time frame.

It was the student's responsibility to gather the resources—computer, Minecraft game, and screen recording software. The student had to explain how he or she would deliver the final product without requiring any purchases or resource gathering by the teacher. His or her solution was using screen-recording software already on his or her computer and YouTube for displaying the work. Sometimes, teachers feel the pressure of not having the skills that the student has for the task. This is unnecessary, rarely possible, and limiting to students taking ownership of their work.

ELIMINATING ASSESSMENT FOG

A danger to single assessments is that sometimes the tool used gets in the way of a student because their skills are limited in the use for work. Consider a test on science or social studies topics where students must explain their understanding of content and evaluate the impact or implications. The test is a series of short answer essay questions. There may likely be some students who are very knowledgeable of what is being tested but fail to demonstrate their depth of knowledge because they have poor writing skills. Or consider word problems or questions that are written at a reading level that is beyond a student's understanding. Reading level becomes an obstacle.

Now some would argue that state tests do not give students alternative options to choose from and are written at levels that are beyond some students. Their logic is that to give choices and/or adapt the language of the test or provide a reader for the test does not prepare students for taking high-stakes tests. They are correct. But the purpose of assessments for learning is to understand what students know and do not know. The data are then reviewed via the FAC to diagnose and plan supports and stretches so that all students can learn. Preparing for test culture as a purpose for assessment creates fog on what students truly have learned.

Assessment fog is *how* assessments are used, creating misinformation of what learners know and do not know. Assessment fog prevents teachers from having clean data for determining what students need. It can lead to students appearing to be exceling in their understanding when the opposite is true. Meanwhile, other students appear to be struggling with content knowledge when the real issue is about their organization skills.

The cause of assessment fog tends to be due to including such factors as assignment logistics assessment values into the academic criteria.

Assignment logistics deal with the guidelines for producing a professional-looking product. Some examples might include:

- writing one's name in the correct space
- using requested color coding
- requiring a paper to be typed, double space, using a specific font and font size, and page length
- meeting submission deadlines
- work is neat
- actively participates and contributes
- follows directions

Such requirements may be important to the overall quality of the work and for efficiently managing collection of assignments, but they do not generally equate to providing data on the academic skills and concepts. When students lack in these skills, coaching is needed. But adding these elements into the academic evaluation creates assessment fog. Could a student who does not follow the teacher's directions show a deep understanding of academic concept and skills? When a student ignores these logistical requirements, can they still turn in evidence that shows a high level of content understanding?

Consider these examples:

Sierra

In social studies, Sierra has a high C. On a recent assignment, she had to label the mid-Atlantic states, cities, and land formations. Her work was assessed at an 80 percent, which indicated that her knowledge might be acceptable. Using the FAC, a problem arose. Every state, city, and land formation was accurately labeled, which indicated 100 percent content accuracy. It soon became clear that Sierra had not followed directions regarding color-coding her labels. Sierra lost points for not following directions. While an important success skill, mixing assessment of following directions with social studies content skills created assessment fog.

How might this situation be addressed?

Matt

In his high school Math course, Matt aces every test. Based on the FAC, his understanding of content is exceptional, yet his course grade is a C minus. Matt does not turn in homework nor does he complete the classwork. When asked, he says that he needs the time to study for his English class.

How should this be addressed so there is accuracy in academic recording, while addressing the non academic issues?

Steve

In Physics, Steve completes all class and homework assignments. He takes notes in class and actively participates in class discussions. Often, he's the only one talking to the teacher. His quizzes tend to be average to below. Due to his hard work, he has a solid B despite poor performances on content tests.

What is needed to clean the data to provide appropriate support?

Avoid assessment tools that indirectly restrict learners from showing what they know and do not know. Weed out the nonacademic factors, so that the data is clean for review through the FAC. For example, logistics requirements, such as header location or formatting requirements, have little to no relationship to assessing a learner's understanding of content knowledge. The skills of following directions, turning in assignments on time, and working well with others may be used as part of the learner experience. That data should be kept in a separate column. Use them. Only keep those scores separate from the academic data.

Some schools report nonacademic factors to parents as college and career readiness (CCR) skills, for example, *manage goals and time*, *work independently*, and *be self-directed learners*.[5] The results are kept and reported separate from the course grade. Schools that do include the nonacademic

CCR skills as part of the academic grade do so as a weighted compartment of the grade. For example, in the New Tech Network,[6] which are project-based learning schools incorporate such a system. Each school determines its weighted system, such as 8 percent for collaboration, 5 percent for responsibility, 10 percent for communication, and 77 percent for academic content. This approach still makes clear where students stand in each category, including academic understanding. The result is that the teacher can review student work and diagnose which students need scaffolds for support and which ones need to be stretched so as not to coast.

FINAL THOUGHTS

Assessments are key to differentiation being targeted and effective for learners. All types of assessments play a role in tracking student progress and needs. Consider that effective teachers spend much time in planning instructional experiences that are intended to support all of their students. With such a time investment, isn't it important to know to what degree that each student responded and his or her level of understanding as a result?

The FAC is a common reflection tool adapted for looking at student data to determine the academic needs for next steps. For the FAC to be effective, the collected data must be clean of assessment fog. Eliminating logistical requirements and behavioral concerns helps one to know exactly what students understand. Other factors can be used to coach students on college and career readiness skills and for strengthening or healing the learning environment—a topic explored in Chapter 6 and Chapter 8.

Consider ways to foster student voice by providing multiple ways for learners to complete assessments. Ensuring that assessments do not create barriers based on skills unrelated to the learning outcome, such as writing an essay to explain a math concept. While writing is important, and students should get frequent practice, have an alternative assessment option so that students have another opportunity that is different to show their understanding.

INVITATIONS TO REFLECTION

Assessment is a huge topic, which is why it is addressed from different angles throughout this book. Within the scope of this chapter, use the lens for differentiation to consider the following questions for implications for learners learning.

1. How do you relate to the definitions for assessment at the start of the chapter? Why is assessment important to learners learning?

2. What parts of the FAC do you feel most comfortable in doing or discussing with others? What parts do you want to delve deeper to improve your practice or to discuss with others?
3. How have you seen or experienced assessment fog, where nonacademic factors were included in the evaluation? How does it make you feel? What changes to practice could have reduced the fog?
4. How might you assess for college career readiness skills separate from the academic evaluation? Choose one from www.P21.org for discussion and common language.
5. Sierra, Matt, or Steve: Which student example raised an "Aha" or affirmation? What connections did you make?
6. What two to three next steps will you take regarding the ideas behind this chapter? Share what changes or additions you would make or communicate.

Crossroad Planning Invitation

- Design or revise a learning experience while factoring the FAC and/or assessment fog.
- Facilitate a discussion with a group or staff on the difference between academic criteria and nonacademic criteria. Use the resource www.P21.org for a list and guide of important skills learners should develop.[7] Review an assessment tool such as a rubric for evidence of both.

Enrichment Option

Create three steps for how you and peers could review assessments for assessment fog.

NOTES

1. Lorna M. Earl. *Assessment as Learning: Using Classroom Assessment to Maximize Student Learning.* Corwin Press, Inc. 2003. pp. 86–87.
2. Assessment for Learning, Education Services Australia, http://www.assessmentforlearning.edu.au/default.asp.
3. Carol Ann Tomlinson. *How to Differentiate Instruction in Mixed-Ability Classrooms,* 2nd edition. ASCD. 2001
4. As an aside, if that is the feeling about the content of this page, skip to the next section or choose a different chapter that is more appropriate.
5. These initiative and self-direction skills and others can be found at P21.org, http://www.p21.org/about-us/p21-framework/266.

6. The New Tech Network (http://newtechnetwork.org) promotes developing students' academic success through project-based learning (PBL) and the college career readiness skills. Its approach to learning promotes innovation in teaching and learning. From personal experience and many classroom observations and coaching of PBL, I can say that PBL is a natural structure for using the differentiation lens.

7. www.SoAllCanLearn.org maintains an update of links for www.P21.org and other resources for your use with staff and students, such as the work by Henrico County Public Schools: TIP Chart—http://blogs.henrico.k12.va.us/21/tip-chart/.

Chapter 4

Informative Assessments
for the Whole Learner

Parents send their best children to school. No child is kept home.
—Virginia Winters, School Improvement Consultant

Instruction can seem hit or miss when trying to reach all students. The more that is known about each student, instruction can be more impactful. The whole child approach by ASCD[1] has been a leader in the conversation for moving from a narrow view of academics to include the important area of skills needed for a citizen of this global community, college, and career. In 2015, the US Congress reauthorized the Elementary and Secondary Education Act under "Every Student Succeeds Act" (ESSA). This replacement of No Child Left Behind (NCLB) follows ASCD on a path to educate the whole child, where they call for the same ideas.[2] Both recognize the importance of students developing the global skills, often called 21st-century skills. The P21.org organization calls these the learning and innovation skills: creativity and innovation, critical thinking and problem solving, and communication and collaboration.[3] The P21 defines other areas that are important to include.

The other commonality with ASCD and ESSA is differentiation. As schools look to follow guidelines from ESSA, with supporting content from ASCD, the whole child approach includes learning preferences and personalized learning as part of preparing students to become productive citizens. Using the differentiation lens provides concrete ways for teachers to include in their practice.

UNDERSTANDING THE LEARNERS IN FRONT OF US

Pictures taken of students might start with snapshots. Based on what is observed, the differentiation lens is zoomed on seeing more about a student.

55

Identifying and understanding the academic strengths and challenges is just the beginning. Why are some students tired or irritated when they first enter the classroom? The answer could be an argument with a loved one, late night of sports and/or work, no breakfast, or that's just the person's personality. Taking snapshots from multiple angles provides a clearer picture of needs.

Using the differentiation lens can help reach more learners. Lessons informed by the students' needs can lead to success in their academic achievement. There are several important elements—some already discussed in other chapters: intentional differentiation, the role of formative assessment, the formative assessment cycle, and assessment fog.

Another key formative assessment element is data about the whole student. The more that is known about each student, the more strategic and personalized the learning experience becomes. Consider the following two examples.

Juan

One Perspective

Juan is usually out of his seat. He's often found socializing with friends, while instruction is happening. When confronted, Juan smiles, which the teacher interprets as he's not taking seriously his continuous disruption of the class. Other times, Juan is completing late work in class when the teacher wants him to focus on the current lesson. The parents never come to parent conferences even when Juan has been sent to the principal's office or served detentions.

Alternative Perspective

Juan is the caretaker of his three younger siblings at home. He feeds them, oversees and does chores, helps them with their homework, and gets them to bed. Juan then plays video games or reads gaming articles to decompress before going to bed. Someday he wants to become a professional gamer. His mother, a single parent, works three jobs to make ends meet. She counts on her eldest child to manage the house in her absence.

Angel

One Perspective

Angel struggles with English and government high school classes. She has low scores on tests and completes only 50 percent of the work. She's in danger of failing both classes. Her teachers have tried talking to her on several occasions about taking her work more seriously—that she needs strong communication skills and an understanding of citizenship—if she hopes to be successful someday.

Alternative Perspective

Angel is a social media darling among her peers. Her video channel and social media following nears one million. The revenues from her video channel provide for her a comfortable living. Between marketing, scripting, and production, she works late at her computer. She's often too tired to do school work once she completes social media tasks for her business. Some of her best work exposes social ills in different communities like lack of good water. School seems like a rote and a tedious obligation in comparison to her world outside of school.

There is so much about students that if teachers only knew could have a positive impact on achievement. Many teachers want to know as much as they can about their students but believe that such a goal has little likelihood due to the many obligations called upon them.

Kyle Schwartz, a third grade teacher, found a way to learn deep truths about her students from a simple homework assignment. She asked students to complete a prompt: "I wish my teacher knew _____." The responses offered insights into the students' lives that might not have normally received.[4] Other teachers have replicated the activity and shared on social media through #IWishMyTeacherKnew,[5] inspired by Kyle's story, which she captured in her book, I Wish My Teacher Knew: How One Question Can Change Everything for Our Kids. Try this simple and insightful approach.[6] Be open to what you learn about them to provide a tighter focus on meeting their needs.

Making learning about every student a priority could have a major impact on their academic success. Providing lessons based just on the academic trends of the group of students in a classroom could have a deeper impact when the whole of each student is factored in the equation for learning.

LEARNING IN AND OUT OF AIRPLANE MODE

The whole student experience in education tends to be like an airplane experience. When passengers get seated for their flight, one of the first messages they receive is to turn off their phones or place them in airplane mode. During the flight, most passengers are disconnected from the world beyond the plane. When the plane lands, usually even before the announcement is made, passengers take their phones out of airplane mode. There is a cacophony of buzzes and rings as phones receive incoming messages and notifications that were waiting for access to be restored.

When students enter school, much of their lives is left outside the doors. The expected focus is academics and achievement. The only student factors considered are where they are academically and any behavior or activities *inside* the building. Family, jobs, responsibilities, and other aspects of a student's life outside of school generally are given little consideration in most instructional planning and experiences. Unlike the staff, the students are kept in airplane mode. This environment makes difficult to attend to the whole child for learning important college and career readiness skills within the guidelines described previously from ESSA and ASCD. When students leave the building, their lives at home and elsewhere return to the forefront. Notifications and messages about needs in their personal lives take over.

CHOICE-BASED STRATEGIES

Eliminating airplane mode and bringing the whole student into instructional considerations can lead to deeper learning experiences. Understanding the whole student impacts how they engage in learning based on readiness, interests, and learning preferences. Content, process, and products become richer with the direct connections that can be made of students to curriculum.

Consider the various choice-based strategies for differentiation needs.[7]

Task Cards

A number of cards, such as four to twelve, are given to students. They are usually kept on a key ring for organization. Each card contains a task to be completed. Students are instructed to complete a number of cards, such as four out of six, or eight out of twelve. In one variation, students must complete all tasks but can pick the order. Sometimes, teachers create several versions of the task cards based on readiness skill levels and assign them to students based on their needs.

Think-Tac-Toe

A classic Think-Tac-Toe is a grid of three rows and three columns, containing nine squares. There is a task to complete in each box. Students must complete three tasks of their choosing that gives them three in a row.

In one variation, the teacher will design different sets of tasks for each row and require students to complete an activity in each row. This approach guarantees that students are exposed to different concepts for the curriculum. Through this variation, students do not need to do three in a row. They just have to complete one task per row.

Another adaptation adds more rows and columns: 4 × 4, 5 × 5, or more. When adding more choices, it's important to ensure that each option provides a respectful quality-learning experience, and that the choices do not become a camouflaged version of skill drills.

Learning Menus

A collection of activities is presented in three sections like a restaurant menu. The work can be assigned to be done as individuals or in groups.

- Appetizers are listed in the first section. Usually included are two to three warm-up tasks. Students choose which appetizer they want to do.
- The main courses are at least two options that focus on the core content for learning. Multiple options allow students to choose which course intrigues them more to complete. Main courses are ideal for a tiering structure, where there are several choices by readiness level.
- Dessert is the final area for completion. These activities enrich or extend the learning. Make them fun so that students want to do them. Not everyone will have time for dessert, depending on how much time the other work takes for them to complete. For those who get done early, dessert options keep them productively engaged.

Learning Centers or Stations

Activities are set up at different locations in the room. Students move to each station to complete tasks. Sometimes tasks are structured around readiness levels. Students may get to choose from options at each station, or they might have to complete tasks at stations that they choose. For example, complete work at three of the four locations.

When students work in learning groups, the activities are opportunities to coach communication and collaboration skills. For example, schools that use project-based learning as a structure to teach curriculum, usually have students work in teams so as to develop the learning and innovation skills. Students communicate and collaborate on understanding the learning outcomes. In heterogeneous groups, all students can use critical thinking and problem solving within a structured learning experience that includes scaffolds for bridging skill gaps. Offered choices in the stations, students choose the means and tools for crafting a creative or innovative product or approach that expresses their understanding.

Learning centers can also be digital. Students follow the same process as the physical version. Some examples include virtual folders created in

Google Drive or a classroom management system. Social network spaces like Pinterest can be used to create the stations.

Each of these activities provides students with choices in what tasks they do. As intentional differentiation, these can be designed by a teacher based on trend data of where learners' academic needs are. Veteran teachers who have taught the lesson in past years, know where students consistently struggle, and can thus predict a similar trend for when they teach the skills in the upcoming lesson. While this is worthwhile as a base for lesson planning, some of the new students from this time around would flourish if the learning experience was personalized to them.

While personalizing for every student would be great for the learner, a few teachers feel up to such a challenge. An effective step is to build differentiation in a lesson first around trends from current student data and informed by past experience of the issues that frequently occur. The next step is to personalize for the students who need more support or challenge beyond the needs of the others.

THE WHOLE STUDENT: FOUR DATA SOURCES THAT INFLUENCE LEARNING

Understanding students based on academic data is a long-standing approach to the science of teaching and learning. Using the formative assessment cycle (FAC), discussed in a previous chapter, helps to think about such data more deeply for meeting the needs of each learner. Academic data alone is not enough information to fully support a student. It's like a doctor basing a diagnosis of symptoms based on what's in the individual's medical history, without considering family history, current lifestyle, and habits.

Humans are complicated. Learning is no easy task. If it was, there would be no need for this book. Consider the whole person based on four data sources: academic, interests, community life, and classroom culture. As with the classic saying, "All roads lead to Rome," incorporating all of these sources leads to more students learning.

Source I: Academic Data

The FAC is only as good as the data used. This is an area that teachers are typically comfortable with in their practice. As discussed in a previous chapter, the FAC provides a reflective frame for educators to look at student data to determine when and where personalized support is needed. Addressing student readiness is greatly influenced by the academic data and it's used through FAC.

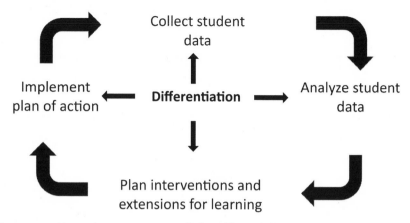

Figure 4.1. Formative Assessment Cycle for Differentiation

For example:

1. Collect academic data on where students are in their understanding of skills and concepts.
2. Analyze and evaluate the causes for gaps and extensions. Diagnose what is needed.
3. Reflect on changes or additions to instructional practices that would better suit the learner. The options may be new and uncomfortable for the teacher.
4. Create and execute a plan of action.

Step 1 is successful when the assessment format supports the skill being assessed. For example, writing an essay explaining science concepts requires scientific knowledge and writing skills. Weak writers may struggle with expressing their science knowledge because, just like an English language learner, the word skills impede their ability to communicate. The solution is to either provide students the opportunity to retake the assessment through other methods so as to establish what content knowledge is known or do not use a format that creates such mismatches.

Where possible, use a learner's strength to show what they know and do not know. Provide the best conditions that allow a learner to express themselves best. Instead of the writing options for the science assessment, provide options like an interview or recording of the student explaining their understanding. There are many ways that students can demonstrate their learning that eliminates assessment fog and provides clear academic data of what students know and do not yet understand.

Source II: Learner Interests

Understand what students know and want to do. Use interest surveys or any self-reflection activity where students share about themselves. Make learning and assessments contextual. Help them see that concepts and skills are present in what they love to do or desire to do. One way to accomplish this is through authentic learning experiences[8] where students explore ideas in context of professional practices (Ron Ritchhart and Mark Church)[9] and through real world applications. Eliminate airplane mode, discussed earlier in this chapter. Including students' learning preferences has a critical impact to student involvement in a task. When an activity is structured in way that helps students find familiarity from what they do in their daily lives, they are more willing to stay tuned in.

Perception is reality. If something looks alien or incomprehensible, they tune out. Understanding that Jane is an artist leads to rich opportunities to make connections of geometry to elements of art. Gregory is a major online gamer. Helping him understand probability and trend lines in a graph through tracking pricing in an auction house to maximize profit will have him drooling to know more.

If Tiffany is a roller-coaster fiend, connecting physics concepts helps her evaluate which roller coasters have the most experience. She can then plan her next awesome adventure. Sunjay loves social media and reads fan fiction. He would love to create complex stories that are told through a collection of characters on Twitter with connecting videos on YouTube.

Empower students by encouraging them to find creative ways to show what they know and do not know through their personal areas of expertise. The teacher does not need to know as much about the tool set that the student wants to use. What matters is that whatever approach the student uses will produce an artifact that aligns to the academic learning outcomes.

Source III: Community Life

A person's life outside of school influences his or her actions and thinking in the workplace. The impact is tremendous as it has a daily influence. What happens at home and community seeps into school. Asking students to forget about life beyond the school walls during class time pays little value to students as people. Only robots can disconnect the past and focus on the present. Students, like their teachers, are constantly influenced by their life beyond the building walls.

Some might say that secondary teachers have a harder time getting to know all of their students, when they may have over 150 students. From personal experience and from visiting many classrooms, the greater number of students makes knowing each student a necessity. A teacher may not know every student with equal depth, but they should know more than just their name, seat location, and grades. Empathy is an important skill to attune to students and *listen* for when they are in need. A simple "good morning" and "how was your weekend" could be all the opening that a student needs.

When Shannon Smith was a principal at Westwood New Tech high school in Michigan, he was well liked and respected by the students. Walking with him in the hallways, he talked to each student by name. He seemed to know something about each person's life whom he spoke to. His students and staff were part of a larger school, so it would be understandable if he didn't know all the students in the building. At the end of each day, he stood outside of the building and spoke to all students by name. When he had to have a tough conversation with students, there was an air of mutual respect that is not always seen in other schools, having visited. Shannon Smith set an example for his staff the importance and value of knowing their students.

The examples of Juan and Angel at the beginning of this chapter also illustrate this reality. Everyone knows a Juan or Angel, probably several. Knowing about a students' life matters to their education.

While teaching an online course for educators, a teacher e-mailed a request. He asked for an extension on assignments. He'd been hospitalized right after the start of the course and was returning after two weeks. There was one and a half weeks remaining in the course. One response could easily have been to have the student drop the course. The other possibility was to give him the extension so that he could get his work done.

Whether a student is the caretaker at home or working the late night shift at a restaurant, a teacher's skills for empathy and readiness to adapt to the student's needs is sometimes needed. Understanding goes a long way in personalizing learning experiences based on what they need.

Source IV: Classroom Culture

Just as a student's home and community life impact his or her state of mind to focus on learning, so does the classroom culture. Students' perception of themselves can change when at school. An added challenge is that students enter the realm of multiple teachers in the course of a day. Even early elementary students may work with teachers in music, art, physical education, and foreign language. It's like working for three to seven bosses. Each has their own expectations. Their style of instruction and mannerisms toward teaching and students will vary. Appropriate behavior and culture expectations in one classroom can be vastly different from another classroom.

Understanding the previous three data sources about students can influence how well they will respond to any teacher in a given classroom. If a student feels like they are welcomed and understood, they may more likely put more effort into supporting the community. If they believe that the environment is negative, they will pay less attention. The reason could be that the teacher is confrontational; student ideas are not valued; or that if a learner comes unprepared because of challenges at home, he or she will be singled out and embarrassed.[10]

Teachers, who are mindful that classroom culture is a shared experience, strive to help students get involved in the shaping of the environment. They monitor themselves as the authoritarian so as to ensure that students feel that their voice is valued and that the focus is on helping them learn. In such classrooms, there is never an airplane mode.

FAIR IS NOT ALWAYS EQUAL: FOUR SOURCES FEED INTO THE WHOLE LEARNER

Three patients see the same doctor. The first person cradles his left arm, which appears to be bent at an abnormal angle.

"Doctor, I think I broke my arm while playing football," she says.

The doctor examines the arm, then says, "Take two aspirin and call me tomorrow morning."

The second person hobbles into the office. He wears bloodstained bandages on both legs. "Doctor, I hurt myself while riding my bike. Please help me."

The doctor examines both legs, without changing the dressings. "Take two aspirin and call me tomorrow morning."

The third person enters the office. She holds a wet towel on her forehead. "Doctor, I have a headache. Can you help me?"

The doctor says, "Take two aspirin and call me tomorrow morning."

When teachers tell this story or conduct this as a role play where the teacher plays the doctor and three students play the patient, the question that's asked of students is: Was the remedy the correct solution for each patient?

The obvious answer is the same, as for the question: Do all learners learn concepts in the same way and pace? In a group of 30 or 40 students in a classroom, is everyone typically at the same academic skill level for what is required of the course? Does teaching skills and concepts the same way during whole group instruction find consistent learning success for each participant?

The overwhelming (and obvious) answer is: no.

Fair instruction is not equal. Learner needs are diverse. While there is overlapping of needs that are common to some part of a group of learners, differentiation is an integral component.

Data from the four assessment sources sheds sunlight on the rich diverseness of learners. Not every lesson needs to be personalized, but parts of each lesson should have some personalized elements for whole group, small groups, and individual learning experiences.

Academics and Readiness Equals Personalization

The academic source informs the readiness of each learner. Support may be structured in mixed-skilled (heterogeneous) groups or by shared-skill level (homogenous). When in the latter type of experiences, students will deal with skills based on what they need. For some, the needs are prerequisite skills and for others the focus is on a more elevated version of the skills. Each person is stretched appropriately to his or her needs.

When learners are grouped heterogeneously, the academic data tell us what scaffolds are needed to give some students the access they need for tackling the complex concepts that "everyone" has the intellectual capacity to address. Like English Language Learners, students who lack prerequisite skills are not dumb. They just have gaps that should be filled or bridged so that they can tackle the cognitively appropriate tasks laid before them.

Academic and Interests Equal Connections

Adding interests into the journey reveals to students how to make sense of concepts that appear to them as alien symbols. Some students thrive with abstract delivery of instruction, such as reading and discussing the laws of motion instead of exploring through experiments of baseball or soccer. Or, studying car crash tests. They understand when a teacher says, "You need to know this concept because it builds from what you've learned previously and connects to what you'll learn later." Other students respond to such statements with looks of incomprehension.

When interests are tied to academics, the lines of code as in the Matrix movies transform into images of experiences that students understand based on their interests. A skateboarder understands slope on a graph because of skateboard parks. Students develop empathy for Brutus as the tragic hero of Shakespeare's *Julius Caesar* when he reflects on difficult decisions he's made in life that impacted others around him. A gamer uncovers the power and price of compromise in historical events like the American Civil War and World Wars I and II based on the dramas that unfold in group play of the combat-based games he or she plays.

Academics, Interests, and Community Equal Self-Confidence

A high school student came to school mid-semester and placed her head down at the start of class. Concerned, the teacher sought to understand the reason. It could not be the lesson as that had not yet started when she rested her head. After a couple of days of unresponsive answers from the student, a parent-student-teacher meeting was scheduled.

The parent explained that the student received a promotion at the fast-food chain store she worked at. She was now the night manager. One responsibility was that when the store closed at 2 a.m., the manager has to supervise the clean up after closing before she could go home. Needless to say, the student was so tired that she could barely stay awake in class.

The teacher instinctively knew not to suggest that the student give up the night manager position because the student and parent would refuse because they believed that the promotion was a boost to the student's self-confidence. The group found another solution that enabled the student to achieve her course credits without being pressured about her job. The student met with the teacher for additional support later in the day. The teacher insisted that the student stay in the morning class. Moving the student would only recreate the problem for another teacher to deal with. Because the student felt supported by the teacher's show of understanding, she agreed to personalized work time later in the day without changing her course schedule.

Empathy is a powerful tonic to turn students into allies about their academic requirements. A student who feels understood and supported will likely do all that's in their power to learn. It may be because they do not want to disappoint the teacher who shows such faith in them. Or, it may be that the teacher's support has paved a pathway so the student can see light beyond the darkness. Interests are part of a student's community. The more that teachers learn about their students, the more inviting are those classrooms to students.

Academic, Interests, and Community Times Classroom Culture Equals Learner Growth

Classroom culture has either a positive (+1) or negative (−1) influence on learning. Simply providing a safe learning environment where students feel that they will get support when and where they need it is a positive multiplier. A basic classroom environment that is positive or negative may exist without the participants being aware of how their actions determining which way the scales tip. Ron Ritchhart addresses these unspoken influences in-depth in *Creating Cultures of Thinking*. Having visited many classrooms, teachers who are driven by content coverage and succumb to the external pressures to stay on pace tend to find themselves frustrated, along with their students who are falling behind.

When a learner's needs are left unmet because of time or a low grade, which they are not allowed to make up, they may perceive the classroom academic environment as cold at best, antagonistic at worst. The multiplier worsens in classrooms where the students are shouldered with the blame for underachieving. When educators make this claim, it is like throwing rocks at a mirror. While students may share in the responsibility for lack of academic success, it is the teacher who has the professional expertise and innovative resources to craft solutions that might eventually turn around the situation.

Positive classrooms hold students accountable for their learning by teachers using the previous three sources to differentiate learning experiences so that each student can learn. If a doctor quit helping a patient after one attempt at a remedy, the public would demand the license to practice. The same goes for the valuable professional in the classroom. Persistence to find a solution by the teacher tells students that they are not allowed to give up on themselves—as a stream of remedies are arriving until an effective solution is found.

Teaching predominantly in a few ways is mainly meeting the needs of the teacher, not the students. Anyone who acknowledges that students learn in different ways and in different paces *and* does not diversify their instruction is not helping anyone. Knowledge is power. Knowing what students need to succeed and then striving to struggle to solutions that meet those diverse needs is what makes teaching heroic and inspirational. The alternative is a loss felt by all stakeholders.

FINAL THOUGHTS

The differentiation lens magnifies the relationship between educator and learner. Students provide a rich perspective about themselves and how they prefer to participate. Teachers can eliminate the airplane mode experience so that students have access to all of their resources. Both should be credited for the successes and take joint responsibility for setbacks. The four assessment sources provide important data in understanding and supporting the whole student. With the whole child gaining more importance through the work of ASCD and the focus given by ESSE, there is much that can be done through the differentiation lens.

Teaching is a calling whose primary purpose it to support learner growth. The job is passionate work that at times gets tugged into the swamps of mandates. Successful teaching is the ability to navigate those treacherous waters while meeting the needs of all students.

INVITATIONS TO REFLECTION

As a result of this chapter, use the lens for differentiation to consider the following questions for a self-guided exploration of your practice and those who you support.

1. How might you use the "I Wish My Teacher Knew _____" activity with students, staff, and colleagues? What might you anticipate learning? https://twitter.com/hashtag/IWishMyTeacherKnew

2. Picture one or two students that you work with of any age, like Juan or Angel. What is the one thing you could learn more about them based on the four assessment sources: academic, interests, community, and classroom culture?
3. Given the concerns with time, how is using the four assessment sources a means to save time in the long term, when it may take more time in the short term?
4. Share one or more strategies for collecting data for one or more sources from the four assessment sources: academic, interests, community, and classroom culture.
5. Why should classroom culture matter when it comes to meeting students' academic needs?
6. What value is there for considering students' community when addressing curriculum?

Crossroad Planning Invitation

• Design or revise a learning experience that includes one of the choice-based options included in this chapter, or that serve a similar purpose.
• Prepare and implement a reflective discussion on choice-based options for students. Generate by the group or staff a list of 20 approaches.
• Review the information about the whole child on the website for ESSE.
    – Generate three focus areas your school or organization could address.
    – List two resources from the site and/or that of ASCD to support the generated focus areas.
    – Pose one question you have based on your research. Share on www. SoAllCanLearn.org.

Enrichment Option

While designing the aforementioned learning experience, factor student information based on the section *The Whole Student: Four Data Sources That Influence Learning*.

NOTES

1. Extensive information can be found at ASCD: Whole child http://www.ascd. org/whole-child.aspx.
2. Educate the whole child by ESSA has informative details at: http://www.educa tethewholechild.org/.
3. The P21.org has many resources that can support the work that schools do under ESSA. For more information, go to http://www.p21.org/our-work/resources.

4. CBS News did a segment about the experience. View it on www.SoAllCan Learn.org. Donna De la Cruz. "What Kids Wish Their Teachers Knew." *The New York Times*. August 31, 2016. http://www.nytimes.com/2016/08/31/well/family/what-kids-wish-their-teachers-knew.html.

5. #IWishMyTeacherKnew includes many sharing of students' responses and teacher reflections. View them at: https://twitter.com/hashtag/IWishMyTeacherKnew. Become inspired, take the risk, and try this with your students and staff.

6. Additional strategies for collecting information from and about students can be found on www.SoAllCanLearn.org.

7. There are many approaches to differentiation via choices. More resources are found at: www.SoAllCanLearn.org.

8. John McCarthy. "Authenticity = Lifelong Learners." Edutopia, December 3, 2015. http://www.edutopia.org/blog/authenticity-equals-lifelong-learners-john-mccarthy. "4 Paths to Engaging Authentic Purpose and Audience." Edutopia, April 13, 2015. http://www.edutopia.org/blog/differentiated-instruction-authentic-purpose-audience-john-mccarthy.

9. Ron Ritchhart and Mark Church. *Making Thinking Visible: How to Promote Engagement, Understanding, and Independence for All Learners*. Jossey-Bass. 2011.

10. Ron Ritchhart. *Creating Cultures of Thinking: The 8 Forces We Must Master to Truly Transform Our Schools*. Jossey-Bass. 2015.

Chapter 5

The Truth about Differentiated Instruction

Do or do not. There is no try.
    —Yoda, *Star Wars: Episode V—The Empire Strikes Back* (1980)

In a middle school in Nashville, Tennessee, grade level teams of teachers met for coaching on differentiation. The teams gathered over several months where they explored instruction and learning through the lens of differentiation and designed strategies to try with their students. One group shared how they used ideas from the three-dimensional instruction protocol in their lessons. They used videos, small group activities, and "field trips" just outside the building as ways for students to explore the academic concepts in nontraditional ways. Several teachers' eyes lit up as they told of the increased level of engagement by their students. It was a moment of optimism and hope.

Only months before, these same teachers had started their journey in a much different mood. Entering the room for their first session about differentiation, they sat with arms crossed, some with papers to grade, or phones out to check messages. Their initial skepticism was palpable. Everyone agreed that differentiation helped students. The phrases "ideal world" and "perfect situation" were used to establish the impossibility of implementing differentiation in the classroom. In this situation, conventional wisdom might suggest that the last thing to do would be add fuel to their justification for why differentiation would not be a fit in their classroom.

Ignoring conventional wisdom, the next question asked of the teachers was: "What are the challenges that make differentiation difficult or impossible?" The list of concerns was long. It can be summed up by six areas that are commonly shared.

1. Differentiation is too difficult to do.
2. There is not enough time to differentiate.

3. Need to prepare for the high-stakes tests by covering all the material.
4. The curriculum is overpacked.
5. Crowded classrooms make differentiation too difficult.
6. How are learning preferences useful?

What follows are responses to these obstacles—how to overcome and move past—so as to empower teachers with differentiation. There are other "obstacles." For these commonly shared challenges, exploring solutions to them can create a constructive momentum fueled by solutions. The results can lead to greater understanding and use of differentiation that makes it possible to overcome other obstacles that may appear.

DIFFERENTIATION IS TOO DIFFICULT

Differentiation is like playing games. In gaming universe, players invest time completing tasks and collecting tools along the way. They accumulate experience points that earn levels, badges, and achievements. High-level players use stronger tools to accomplish more challenging tasks with greater expertise.[1] Differentiation has many levels for implementation. The beginning level is simple: Understanding one's practice is intuitive (in the moment).

Like a gamer, educators who invest time in reflection on practice around differentiation level up by exploring intentional differentiation, which is where preplanning occurs. Teachers analyze students' needs based on assessment data and craft learning experiences that meet their needs. The Dorothy Principle[2] is a reminder that teachers have the core skills to differentiate. They need to use the differentiation lens to see the possibilities.

Differentiation starts with reviewing assessment data on what learners know and do not know. Once a learner's needs are identified, appropriate steps can be planned for instruction that may range from whole class to small groups, to individual experiences. Remember Lorna Earl's description of assessments:

> Differentiation is making sure that the right students get the right learning tasks at the right time. Once you have a sense of what each student holds as "given" or "known" and what he or she needs in order to learn, differentiation is no longer an option; it is an obvious response.[3]

The reality of every day common sense best practice is expressed in the second sentence, "Once you have a sense of what each student holds as 'given' or 'known' and what he or she needs in order to learn . . ." When professional practitioners (teachers) identify who is struggling and who is not receiving appropriate challenge, their instinct is to find out why, just as a competent doctor does for a patient. Once the needs are identified, teachers, like doctors, have a professional and moral obligation to address the needs of

Table 5.1. Leveling Up Differentiation

Levels of Implementation	Description of What Differentiation Looks Like
One	Teacher practice is intuitive rather than intentional. Student needs are met during lessons only when the needs appear and are recognized by the teacher. For example, students not asking questions, lay heads on the table, little to no activity on the assignments, limited participation/engagement. Supports may be organically developed.
Two	Teacher practice is mostly intuitive with some intentional influences. Student needs are met during lessons as the needs appear, based on observations and planned formative assessments. Some support resources are readily available and provided to students as needed, based on previous experiences from teaching the lesson concepts.
Three	Teacher uses intentional planning to begin supporting intuitive practice but may be used infrequently. Teacher reflects on assessment data as a means to develop and/or align resources that support the common learning gaps by students during the lesson. Data analysis is mostly group trends, rather than based on individual needs.
Four	Teacher uses intentional planning to target support for crossroad lessons. Resources are developed and provided to address academic growth for struggling and advanced students based on their needs. The focus of support may occur prior to key assessments, or after the assessment has taken place.
Five	As part of intentional planning, the teacher explicitly uses the elements of differentiation. The teacher can explain the specific connections of their differentiation practices to content, process, and/or products. Usage may occur at least twice a week. Assessment data are used frequently to inform decisions for differentiating instruction. Three-dimensional instruction occurs at least once a week.
Six	Instructional use of content, process, and products is an integrated part of planning. For example, process experiences increase to two or more times during a lesson. Use of readiness, interests, or learning preferences is being intentionally explored to increase the quality of learning experiences. Individual assessment data are beginning to be used for some opportunities for personalizing or individualizing the learner experience. Three-dimensional instruction occurs frequently each week where needed.

(Continued)

Table 5.1.   (Continued)

Levels of Implementation	*Description of What Differentiation Looks Like*
Seven	Intentional planning happens frequently as part of the natural process of preparing learning experiences. Student voice begins to have an influence on instruction based on data collection for readiness, interests, and learning preferences. Students experience learning experiences where they are actively working alone and in groups based on their identified needs and interests.
Eight	Intentional planning and intuitive support is heavily influenced by the needs identified by learners. The students decide or co-plan some of their learning experiences within the areas of content, process, and/or products. Teacher and students use the elements of differentiation to craft learning experiences that support the curriculum outcomes. Assessment data are used frequently for ongoing teaching, coaching, and assessing by both teachers and students.
Nine	Intentional planning and intuitive support are fluid and occur daily as part of the natural course of teaching and learning. The lead role of learning is interchangeable between students and teacher. The student may provide the direction based on their interests and learning preferences, while the teacher leads on cocreating experiences based on student readiness. Assessment data are used to adapt, adjust, and/or change learning experiences where needed, based on the curriculum outcomes. Teacher and students collaborate as co-learners for innovative methods to meet learning needs through the lens of differentiation.

those under their care. Choosing to ignore the educational health needs is the equivalent of professional malpractice.

Every teacher has the capacity to differentiate instruction. The tools of assessments and reflection on practice are available to meet the most basic needs for implementation. With experiences, professional growth, trial and error, and reflection on practice, educators can level up their differentiation skills to have an even greater impact so that all can learn.

THERE IS NOT ENOUGH TIME TO DIFFERENTIATE

Teaching and learning are complex processes. Time is needed for educators to develop expertise in their practice for the benefit of students. Differentiation done well requires ongoing practice, patience, and time for a teacher to deepen his or her practices so all can learn. Fortunately, intentional differentiation can be practiced at a basic level where teachers anticipate possible learning challenges, based on previous experiences teaching the same content. The time commitment for differentiation can be minimal for intuitive practice as those happen in the moment of instruction. Basic intentional practices can start simply with the planning of basic needs for a crossroad lesson on a weekly basis. For example, support vocabulary building with a Frayer Model. Students develop an understanding of terms from four different perspectives.

Using the Frayer Model is a quick starter to support vocabulary development. With more experience and professional learning, there are many

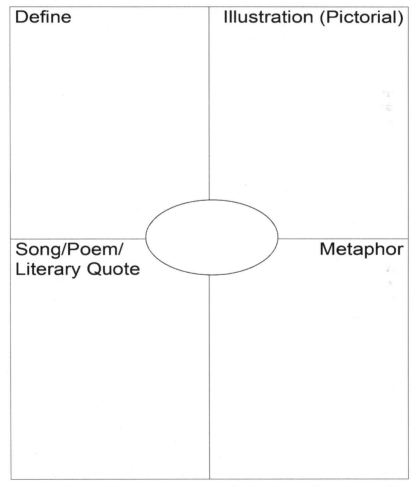

Figure 5.1.   Frayer Model: Vocabulary. Visit www.openingpaths.org for more resources on Differentiated Instruction[4]

Traditional: Enter the Vocab Word in the center circle.
Complete the sections of this chart and be prepared to share.

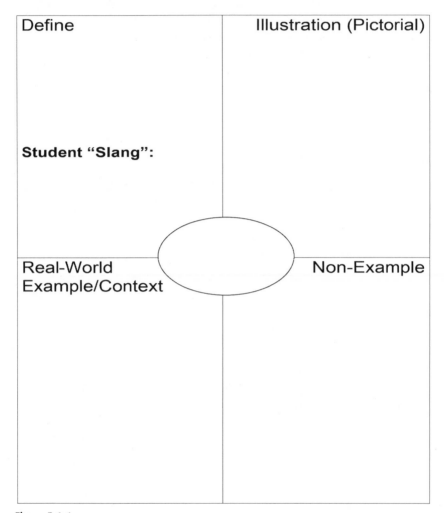

Figure 5.1-1

other strategies that support vocabulary development that may have a deeper impact on learner growth.

Time Value versus Quantity

"Slow is smooth, and smooth is fast."[5] Skill development in any field takes time, understanding, and practice. Taking time to understand the nuances of a skill can lead to applications under fast-paced conditions. For example, learning how to dribble a football (American soccer) is a slow and steady process. Players practice over and over standing still, then walking, then jogging, and then against other players who challenge them. It is not until the skill is mastered that they can run *and* maintain control of the dribble with finesse that makes the action look easy.

While this idea of going slow to develop smoothness in skill makes sense, a commonly expressed concern in education is that time is limited for content coverage, which makes going slow seem like wishful thinking. In this scenario, teachers learn about the use of high-impact strategies and instructional techniques that they believe will improve student achievement. Research may support the approaches, such as found in What Works Clearinghouse,[6] and teachers can see the results are favorable. However, the time required to implement such strategies is perceived as too much.

For example, running a reading comprehension protocol like Save the Last Word, Say Something, or Socratic Seminar can help all students gain more comprehension of important ideas than one person reading aloud while everyone listens.[7] The time to complete these protocols can be anywhere from 20 minutes to 50 minutes depending on the variation of the protocol used—whereas a read aloud might take only 10 minutes. From a quantitative perspective, it's hard to argue against 10 minutes, which leaves 10 to 40 minutes to do other instruction. From a value perspective, the protocols require active engagement with the text through reflective thinking and dialogue in a group. The read aloud is a mostly passive experience by the group, while the one person is reading.

Value of time is based on what experiences will best enable students to build the needed understanding. Some higher levels of differentiation implementation do take more time in the short term. But when the experience matches the learner needs with lasting results, fewer students may have gaps in understanding. The potential long-term effect can be that fewer students require reteaching because of the early investment of time. One example is timely feedback that is specific and constructive (see Chapter 1 regarding feedback).

Time is a key consideration when planning instruction. The important filter is "what do learners need," and not "where in the curriculum does the time table say the class should be." The negative result of content coverage is that more learners fall behind and disengage. The outcome of this situation is that more time is needed to reteach material that was never learned the first time, and now there may be little to no time to get learners to catch up. Go slow to become smooth, be smooth to go fast.

THE CURRICULUM IS OVERPACKED

A curriculum with so much content to address is a challenge both of time and of pedagogy. When time is limited, pedagogy or approaches to instructional practices can lead to teachers feeling like they are plugging holes in an overflowing content dam. The temptation is to revert to content coverage, whereby, the teacher takes center stage. In this scenario, the driving force becomes the teacher's instructional pace to deliver the curriculum rather than students' learning achievement. The tools generally used are

- Presentations

  The teacher delivers content through lectures and videos that impart information that is considered important to know. The focus is on how much content can be communicated within a prescribed time frame. Students may be expected to take notes but are given insufficient to no coaching time for developing proficient note-taking skills and related reflection strategies, as that decreases time for content delivery.
- Worksheets

  Worksheets are generally used for collecting information from resources (i.e., textbooks) or practice of concepts (i.e., equations). It can be the equivalent of a lecture through writing. One challenge with worksheets is the tendency for students to tackle surface-level questions that require little to no in-depth critical thinking. Another challenge occurs when the work is not reviewed by students for analysis and revisions. Feedback on such work could elevate the experience, but such comments require so much time that teachers may not be able to sustain it on a daily basis. The result is that students may view these assignments as a daily checklist to complete, turn-in, and forget.
- Teacher-led Q&As

  On the surface, this approach may be surprising to be part of such a list. This approach typically follows the initiation/response/evaluation (IRE) communication pattern or the initiation/response/follow-up (IRF) communication pattern.[8] Watch a session in action and its problems are revealed. The scene is quite common: The teacher asks a question. Waits. Calls on a student or a student volunteers to answer the question. Once the answer is given, the teacher elaborates or asks a new question. The process repeats for as long as the activity runs. The teacher is the most active by having the most engaged talking opportunities. A handful of students answer the questions, but in reality, that small group of participants might have one or two talking opportunities. Meanwhile the majority of students are passive participants. The benefit of these experiences is that the teacher can ensure that key content gets covered.

If such practices have no assurances that understanding by most to all students, then why are they so popular? They reassure educators that the curriculum gets covered as much as possible.

Teachers want their students to succeed, yet may feel unsure as to address two competing needs: ensure that all students learn and cover all curriculum expectations. Differentiation helps the first need but not the second. Yet, if the focus is on ensuring that all learners achieve, then overpacked curriculum can be made manageable. Consider these questions:

1. If curriculum coverage is incompatible with learners developing sustained understandings, then what components are truly nonnegotiable for understanding?
2. Which knowledge-based needs to be memorized versus accessed?
3. What curriculum must be taught in a time-based chronology or in a thematic- or concept-based approach?

The answers are varied, depending on the innovative approaches that educators are willing to take when the priority is students learning. Examples include inquiry-based learning, authentic learning experiences, design thinking, Response to Intervention (RtI), restorative justice, STEAM, project-based learning, genius hour, MakerSpace, career, technical and engineering (CTE), Montessori, constructivist-based learning, and magnet academies. All of these structures provide a frame to address curriculum and differentiation where the learner is at the center.

NEED TO PREPARE FOR THE HIGH-STAKES TESTS BY COVERING ALL THE MATERIAL

Differentiation does not guarantee success on tests. Some have asked, "Why should I differentiate instruction when tests are not differentiated? Doesn't that create a disconnect for students in preparing for (high-stakes) tests?"

The answer to the first question goes to the purpose of differentiation. Without such support, students who are falling behind, find themselves with an insurmountable gap in understanding that may lead them to shutting down. Scan a classroom for students with their heads on their desks or eyes looking anywhere but where the instruction is happening. These are individuals who are disconnected from the instruction, which may be due to their feeling lost in the content—readiness and/or learning preferences—or feeling disinterested—interests.

Using differentiation as a lens for preplanning instruction, informed by learner needs (intentional differentiation) can help students have growth in their learning. This may lead to narrowing gaps in understanding. If students find success where there was once unresolved frustration, there can be more opportunities for learning engagements. A possible result is that there will be students who close the learning gap sufficiently to have greater improvement on high-stakes tests, which may not have occurred without personalized support.

A student who is two years behind may attain a year's growth that they would normally not have gotten without differentiation, as the following example will show. This may have a varied impact on the high-stakes test. Some learners will close the gap enough to make a noticeable difference, while others whose level of understanding skills and concepts were so low that any significant improvements may not register on a grade level assessment.

Take for example, guided reading (Pinnell and Fountas)[9] where students work in readiness reading levels. Students who are reading two to four reading levels below grade level could have dramatic improvements that close the skill gap, but they still may not be at grade level. Should guided reading be abandoned? Obviously, no. For struggling learners who are far behind the proscribed grade level, completely closing the gap requires a systemic relay approach. Each teacher hands-off students who have narrowed the achievement gap to the next teacher, who continues the process until the students surpass the finish line. Where such systems do not exist, through persistent differentiation teachers will know that they are fulfilling their calling.

The question of high-stakes tests not being differentiated may be a concern to advocate to state and national organizations to make a change in their practice. Whether or not that occurs should not stop teachers from ensuring that learners are growing in their skills and understanding of the curriculum. There is, however, a way to differentiate in preparation for high-stakes tests.

Game-Day Scenarios

In arenas of competition, in athletics, gaming, and academics, there are common practices for success. For example, in basketball, a coach will run the team through various scenarios to practice game-day situations. Practice an offense that runs off clock time before taking a shot, running a full court press defense under the condition of being down 4 points with 60 seconds remaining, playing out pass plays to in-bound the ball under the hoop and along the court sideline. Why practice these scenarios? Wouldn't it be more valuable to spend more time on layups, jump shots, passing, dribbling, and memorizing plays?

Coaches include these scenarios so that the players get comfortable with the plays and ball handling under game conditions. The expectation is that by applying the skills and concepts in practice, in the actual game will feel more normal. The same can be true for academics.

Consider how students could draft essays for an upcoming assignment under test-like conditions, as was related by teachers in Columbia, South

Carolina, and Clarkston, Michigan.[10] Within the projected time frame of the test, students write first drafts of essays. For example, if the essay time is 30 minutes, students take 5 minutes to outline ideas so as to organize their thoughts before writing. Then take 15 minutes to draft the essay using the outline as a guide for coherence. The final 10 minutes is used to revise and polish.

The time frame could be longer, such as 90 minutes. It depends on the time given by the specific high-stakes test. The teacher coaches the students during each session, providing guidance and feedback in the moment based on how the students follow the structures. Differentiation is used based on the particular needs of students as addressed in the moment (intuitive) of the work and later as follow up coaching based on results from previous practice (intentional).

Because the experience is not an actual assessment, the learning opportunity can have a positive impact on learning and understanding of the test conditions. Follow this approach four to six times during the year, and students build up their skills and stamina. Now when the high-stakes test is implemented, students are more experienced with the test conditions.

This is true with any testing structure—multiple choice, reading comprehension, and math solutions. Use the practice time for students to explore the related steps, share struggles and strategies, and then practice new solutions. Involve students in the thinking and strategizing. Game on!

CROWDED CLASSROOMS MAKE DIFFERENTIATION TOO DIFFICULT

Crowded classrooms can be relative to different school levels and situations. A classroom of 30 high school students may be manageable, whereas the same amount of kindergartners or first graders is a significant issue. One hundred university students may appear less concerning than forty-four high school students in a room with thirty-eight chairs.

Another factor to consider is that secondary teachers may work with "approximately" 30–45 students in one course. If they teach five courses, their instructional responsibilities include 150–225 learners on a daily basis. Face time with secondary students during on-site courses tends to be approximately 45–50 minutes per day. Elementary teachers may work with 20–30 students, which might seem an easier gig than the significantly high caseloads of secondary.

It is illusionary to believe that elementary teachers have it much easier because they have only one group of students to focus on the entire day. Consider that they are responsible for all four core content areas: math, history, science, and language arts—that's the equivalent of teaching four courses. They may also handle other responsibilities such as recess, break-fasts, lunches, and the arts depending on school budgets. A large number of students under a teacher's caseload is a challenging learning environment regardless of grade level.

Large numbers of students at any level can feel overwhelming. Under such stressful conditions, it's important to stay focused on the primary purpose: student learning and not curriculum coverage. Having taught in classrooms with large number of students, it quickly became clear that differentiation is of greater necessity if the goal is to ensure that all students can learn and grow.

The temptation is to bend the work of curriculum coverage through solely teacher-led instruction, because then the instructor can control the pace of information delivery. One result is that the teacher is able to stay on pace with their peers, and with what is believed to be the appropriate timeline for learning progression. The reality is that delivering content on a prescribed curriculum timeline does not equate to learning success. Many teachers have shared anecdotally their frustration with keeping pace, while at the same time noting the students who did not pass assessments. Some of the teachers created a support plan to possibly spiral instruction, scheduled coaching time, and/or included reteaching. But many of the teachers moved on with the lessons, because the messages by their school leadership was interpreted as staying on pace with the other teachers was more important than addressing the growing learning gap of their students.

Learners develop understanding at their own pace. A well-designed curriculum plan that is timed like a bus schedule crumbles in the face of learners who do not "get it" the first 2 times or because a group of students demonstrate that they are far ahead of the time table. Differentiation is even more of a necessity when classrooms are crowded.

The best solution for teaching a large, possibly overcrowded, class is to make the numbers smaller. In such instances, a class of 40 students put into teams of 4 shrinks the instructional focus on to 10 learning groups.

Base the groups by readiness level or create mixed-skilled groups where everyone can support the learning outcomes. There are many strategies that can be adapted for meeting of needs by students grouped for readiness or mixed-skill levels. Some include:

• Centers: physical or virtual via blended approaches
• Think Dots and Task Cards
• Learning menus
• RAFTS and similar writing prompts

One important key for teachers is to be deliberate in how the groups are formed for a specific purpose.

Form Groups of Students Based on Their Readiness Levels

There are times when students need to work on concepts and skills where they share common needs for understanding. Guided reading is a classic example where students are grouped by reading levels for common skill needs. Where guided reading is a systemic approach, teachers can use grouping strategies for different moments where such instruction could be the difference for learner growth. During a science or social studies activity, students could be in reading level groups to develop comprehension of facts and concepts from articles chosen for their appropriate leveled comprehension by the student groups.

During math work, students could be grouped with like-skills to collaborate on completing simple or complex tasks around such topics as quadratic equations or two- to three-digit multiplication. Groups are assigned based on the conceptual level of understanding they currently have so as to grow to the next levels.

The ASCD, which has a wealth of resources on differentiated instruction, has a video that shows elementary students learning how to tell time on an analog clock.[11]

One group works on telling time to the minute, while another tells time in five minute chunks, and a final group works on telling time to the quarter hour.

Grouping by readiness serves the dual purpose of enabling students to give and receive support to and from their peers as they collaborate on shared understanding of the learning experience. Also, the teacher is freed from the front of the room to provide just-in-time coaching to students, both those who struggle and others who need the next level of understanding.

Form Groups of Students with a Mix of Skills, with a Shared Interest

The value of grouping students with a mixture of readiness levels is that all students bring value to the table. Students have academic strengths and learning preferences to opens up different lenses on the work. What should be avoided is forming learning groups where lesser-skilled students feel that they have nothing to contribute and more skilled members feel that they must carry the work load. In such instances, little learning of academics may take place.

A first step for venturing into mixed-skill groups is to provide tasks that address learning preferences. From the previous list in this chapter, use Think Dots or Task Cards. Each task addresses the learning outcome from a different learning preference, which allows the entire team to explore each task together, and ensuring that some members will have a take on how to complete the tasks.

Think Dots

Global Studies—Understand that Class Structures can connect people and divide them.

II. Geographic Perspective: 1.1, 2 & 3

Instructions: Complete all six items on separate paper in order or randomly. You may use any resources from books to websites. For each task, each person will take on one of the following roles. Everyone must participate in each role at least once:

- **Facilitator:** reads the task and make sure that everyone gets to speak.
- **Scribe:** makes a written record of the group's work.

- **Summarizer:** States the final answers for a task before the group can move on to a new task.
- **Investigator:** Leads group on fact checking for accurate answers.

Define the following words: - Feudalism - Caste System - Cliques - Popularity - Filial Piety - Chivalry - Bushido ●	Use a T chart to list 2–4 benefits and challenges of Feudalism or Caste System ●●	List 2–4 responsibilities of warriors following the code of Chivalry or Bushido to the common people. ● ● ●
Draw a picture or graphic organizer (e.g., tree, web) that represents the social structure of groups in your school (e.g. teachers, parents, athletes, dancers, skaters). ●● ●●	List 2 songs where one represents an idea of Filial Piety and one does not. Discuss and cite at least one lyric from each to support your choices. ●● ●● ●●	Aliens arrive from a distant planet. What would you tell them about your community that brings people together or creates unfairness? Cite a specific example through a blog entry, dialogue script, or poster. ●●● ●●● ●●●

List the lesson's objective and related assessment, before developing the Think Dots for best results.

Figure 5.2. Think Dots Example

Another way to think of these groups is as study teams or thought partners who collaborate on the curriculum tasks that are typically assigned. Yet when creating work for these teams, the learning experiences can be more effective when the task formation includes an understanding of each student. Using learning preferences, interests, and even readiness to form the learning tasks helps provide teams a way to tackle skills and concepts as a team. From the perspective of class sizes, the support of learners is more manageable for teachers when they are not thinking in terms of 30 or 40 individuals, but instead with teams of 3 or 4 students, teachers are looking at the more manageable 10 groups.

HOW ARE LEARNING PREFERENCES USEFUL?

While most can agree that each person is unique in how he or she thinks and responds to external stimuli, when it comes to learning preferences there is disagreement about its existence. Many classroom teachers have shared about the differences in their students in terms of how they tackle assignments, take instruction, and process their thinking. They see learner diversity on a daily basis.

Yet the opposite position should not be ignored. Respected researchers, such as John Hattie and Gregory Yates, have reviewed the literature on studies done about learning styles in their book *Visible Learning and the Science of How We Learn*. Of those reviewed who argue against learning styles, they address the topic with a clarity on the history of how learning styles use evolved and the *specific* areas of usage that can create problems for instructional application. They state:

> However, in considering the various learning styles posited, we reach a clear conclusion: that there is not any recognized evidence suggesting that knowing or diagnosing learning styles will help you to teach your students any better than not knowing their learning style.[12]

This conclusion was based on a review of many studies that came out with a similar outcome. They specify further on, by stating:

> In other words, it is nonsense to hold the idea that some of your students can be classified as visual learners whereas others, within the same class, are auditory learners. There simply is no known validity to making any such classifications on the basis of either neurology or genuine behavioral performance.[13]

They raise criticism that needed to be addressed. The second quote relates to the use of classification of learners as either visual, auditory, or kinesthetic, or VAK assessments. Such tests started in 1917 for identifying needs in the military. This was developed over the years with the intent of matching individuals to occupations, first in the military, and later for general consumption. This is referred to as the *match process*, which included the IQ test. Over the years, this matching process seemed to not be effective for matching.

One problem is that these types of assessment are used to categorize people as, mainly, one type of learner, and so limited from doing kinds of work that uses other learning styles. A result might be to develop activities that compose of a different VAK, and then assign them to students based on their *identified* learning style. Such an action would be a grave error.

The appropriate response to this concern is to look at learners as benefiting from many or all the learning styles descriptors. Students can benefit from learning experiences that include a variety of learning styles, just by incorporating into lessons. When options are developed that focus on one learning style per task choice, let the students choose what they want to do. From personal experience, learners tend to choose the task that interests them. Sometimes the task aligns with their expressed preferences, which can be a win. It is important that students not be denied the learning experiences that might appear to be a mismatch. Instead, through the experience, students could have the opportunity to see things from a different perspective. Either way, failing to complete a task will not be because of learning preferences, which is the seasoning. Failure is either a flaw in the instructional planning or an opportunity for student growth.

The second problem the authors raise is the collection of data through inventories or other response systems. These are found to be less than accurate. At best, the responses offer a perspective of the tested person's self-perception of themselves. The results are subjective, which makes assigning people into learning styles a very difficult task.

A workable solution is to use the information as one of several sources for getting to know each student. Might you discover through observations that what the learner said is his or her preference does not match how he or she actually experience learning? Yes. Update the notes about that student for future use.

One important step for teachers is to change their language (Ron Ritchhart)[14] from learning styles to learning preferences. Learning styles can limit students to categories for what they can and cannot do. Learning preferences encourages students to explore what works for them, and discover how those preferences can change over time or depending on the circumstance. Learning preferences should be used as a means to know students beyond the surface information. The authors, while cautioning teachers from using inventories, do acknowledge that:

> Some of your students are more intellectual, some are more anxious, some react quickly, and others plan more carefully. Some tackle new areas with confidence, but others appear less optimistic.[15]

The authors go on to recognize the benefits of exploring content from multiple learning perspectives:

> Of course, all students benefit from instruction that encompasses analyzing images, hearing words, and acting out key aspects. But this is not what is being suggested by the match hypothesis.[16]

There can be agreement that learners are unique and can all benefit from a variety of experiences that used different modalities for learning. For example, consider the three-dimensional instruction approach (Chapter 2) for offering a variety of perspectives in a lesson.

Explore the use of learning profile cards (Chapter 9) to collect anecdotal data from the students. The information can be used as insights for what to include as part of the learning. They can also be used to thoughtfully form student teams for promoting agency skills, such as student voice, choice, collaboration, and communication.

The learning profile cards intentionally seek to collect data from two to three different learning styles or inventories approaches. It is a form of cross-training. Using two or more different approaches helps teachers to look at students as the multifaceted complex learners that they are.

Using the differentiation lens means viewing learners and supporting them from as many angles as can be conceived.

FINAL THOUGHTS

The many concerns over challenges that exist in education have less to do with differentiation than with the school structures. Differentiation of instruction does help students achieve learning. This is seen through practices that are research-based.[17] Any practices that teachers successfully implement to meet the needs of students can be differentiated, if based on effective use of assessments and reflections about the data—as discussed regarding the formative assessment cycle.

The more challenging that a school or classroom setting becomes because of barriers of time, mandates, class size, or other obstacles that seem to threaten the ability to provide students learning support, the greater is the need for differentiation.

Certainly, the obstacles must be overcome. Solutions must be tried through various trials until the conditions improved. Students as the center of instructional decisions must be *the* lens for all such decisions. Unfortunately, student-centered focus is not always the practice by policymakers who have less understanding than those who must implement their directives. However, teachers as trained professionals do influence what happens inside the classroom, both the physical and virtual locations. As this chapter sheds light on the possibilities for overcoming some of the commonly expressed challenges, find inspiration to look inside one's toolbox and use or adapt instructional strategies and frameworks for addressing the current obstacle that stands in the way of learning.

The foundational reality is that students are in the teacher's presence every school day. What teachers do to meet learner needs with full commitment to action is valuable. Succeeding means students gain. Failing is an opportunity to reflect on student data and teaching practices so as to find student success in the next attempt. To paraphrase Yoda in the *Empire Strikes Back*, "Do."

INVITATIONS TO REFLECTION

As a result of this chapter, use the lens for differentiation to consider the following questions for a self-guided exploration of your practice and those whom you support.

1. Describe the difference in approach between teacher-centered content coverage and student-centered content learning? Which do you practice or see practiced more? Which three steps could you and peers follow to travel the paths of student-centered content learning?
2. Of the challenges explored in this chapter, which one do you understand most how to overcome? How would you explain it in a different way—story or analogy—to someone who feels stuck?
3. Of the challenges explored in this chapter, which one do you still struggle with? Explain the heart of your struggle, which prevents finding a way to differentiate? Now evaluate how the heart of your struggle looks like from the perspective of teacher-centered coverage versus student-centered learning.
4. Make a list of your top five obstacles, which may or may not include those discussed in this chapter. Identify which obstacles directly impact instructional practice and learning experiences versus having a greater impact

on the management and logistical work of the teacher, such as turning in weekly lesson plans or giving common assessments. Evaluate the former for strategies that place students at the center of learning decisions.

5. Consider Lorna M. Earl's two sentence definition of differentiation:

Differentiation is making sure that the right students get the right learning tasks at the right time. Once you have a sense of what each student holds as "given" or "known" and what he or she needs in order to learn, differentiation is no longer an option; it is an obvious response.

What implications does the second sentence have on the responsibility of teachers for overcoming any obstacle that may stand in the way of student learning? How might this quote be applied to the current practices of you and your peers?

6. How might you use learning preferences over learning styles to provide instruction that supports learner needs?

Crossroad Planning Invitation

- Make a list of three concrete steps for how you will overcome one of the challenges explored in this chapter.
- Facilitate a group or staff dialogue regarding the challenges shared in this chapter. Consider using a jigsaw approach or use a reflective reading protocol, such as Say Something, Save the Last Word for Me, or the Spider Discussion.[18]

Enrichment Option

Choose a challenge addressed in this chapter. Create a digital presentation or explanation for how your colleagues can overcome the challenge. Publish or share your ideas with your peers.

NOTES

1. These qualities for playing games are also used in the education world, known as *gamification*. Read this Edutopia article, "Gamification & Differentiation: Meeting the Needs of All Learners" by John McCarthy.

2. The Dorothy Principle is explained in Chapter 2.

3. Lorna M. Earl. *Assessment as Learning: Using Classroom Assessment to Maximize Student Learning.* Corwin Press, Inc. 2003. pp. 86–87.

4. The Frayer Model original developers are: Frayer, D., Frederick, W. C., and Klausmeier, H. J. (1969). A Schema for Testing the Level of Cognitive Mastery. Madison, WI: Wisconsin Center for Education Research.

5. This quote has many references, mostly in the military for skill development.

6. The What Works Clearinghouse has researched supported instructional strate-gies. All can be adapted using the differentiation lens. http://ies.ed.gov/ncee/wwc/.

7. Find links and explanations of these resources at www.SoAllCanLearn.org.

8. Both concepts, IRE and IRF, can be found online. A starting place would be the glossary on the Annenberg Learner site: https://www.learner.org/workshops/tfl/glossary.html. Follow this with looking at *Guided Instruction* by Douglas Fisher and Nancy Frey. Here's an excerpt from their book: Chapter 2. Questioning to Check for Understanding http://www.ascd.org/publications/books/111017/chapters/Questioning-to-Check-for-Understanding.aspx.

9. Gay Su Pinnell and Irene C. Fountas. *Research Based for Guided Reading as an Instructional Approach.* 2010. http://teacher.scholastic.com/products/guidedreading/pdf/2.0_InYourClassroom/GR_Research_Paper_2010.pdf. *Guided Reading: The Romance and the Reality.* http://www.heinemann.com/fountasandpinnell/supportingmaterials/fountaspinnell_revdreadingteacherarticle12_2012.pdf.

10. This writing structure was successfully used as related by an English teacher in a middle school from Richland County School District Two in Columbia, South Carolina, and my own teaching experience as part of the high school English Depart-ment at Clarkston Community Schools in Clarkston, Michigan.

11. Instructional Strategies for the Differentiated Classroom, Part 1 DVD and Facilitator's Guide, ASCD. http://shop.ascd.org/Default.aspx?TabID=55&ProductId=1558&Instructional-Strategies-for-the-Differentiated-Classroom-(1

12. John Hattie and Gregory C. R Yates. *Visible Learning and the Science of How We Learn.* 2013. p. 176.

13. Hattie and Yates. *Visible Learning and the Science of How We Learn*, p. 179.

14. Ron Ritchhart. *Creating Cultures of Thinking: The 8 Forces We Must Master to Truly Transform Our Schools.* 2015.

15. Hattie and Yates. *Visible Learning and the Science of How We Learn*, p. 180.

16. Hattie and Yates. *Visible Learning and the Science of How We Learn*, p. 181.

17. Refer to the appendices for looking at how research-based practices can be dif-ferentiated. It is important to keep in mind that any instructional strategy that a teacher finds highly effective can be adapted for differentiated experiences.

18. These resources can be found at www.SoAllCanLearn.org.

Chapter 6

Learner Voice Matters

> I like that it [Innovation Days] was student-led, because when we were
> done, we could say that we [students] put it together. Teachers took a step
> back, allowing students to step up and do the work. This gave us pride in
> the end result, knowing that we pulled it off.
> —Jada McCarthy, high school sophomore

At Ardis New Tech High School in the spring of 2014 and 2015, there was
a student-run event called Innovation Days. This two-day event was inspired
by an idea from a Google practice that was described in Daniel Pink's book,
Drive. Students chose a project idea that they wanted to explore—develop a
unique approach or new idea. The classrooms were assigned based on different content areas, English, Science, Math, Social Studies, Music, Art, and
Technology. Teachers rolled up their sleeves to assist and mentor based on
the direction that students wanted to take their ideas. In one room, a group of
eight students used drum sticks on various objects to create a unique sound,
while one student led on a drum kit. The rhythms and sounds produced were
amazing.

Other examples included:

- built a motorized vehicle
- drafted a book on scientific phenomenon
- explored building architecture through Minecraft, an open sandbox game
- crafted works of art

After a day and a half of exploration and inquiry, students presented their
efforts to the school. Several locations were used as presentation sites so that

multiple talks could occur simultaneously. Students, alone and in groups, presented their efforts to an audience of their peers, teachers, and guests.

Both years, a group of students led the development and implementation of the event under the mentorship of a teacher. The group called themselves, Student Voice.

THE REALMS OF DIFFERENTIATION

Readiness, interests, and learning preferences are elements that learners share influence with teachers. As teachers craft the lesson experience based on content, process, and/or product, they use the differentiation lens based on how student data inform on readiness, interests, and/or learning preferences. Students approach these lessons and tasks as invitations to participate:

Readiness: Is the experience structured so that the stretch to learn is matched to the student?

Vygotsky's "Zone of Proximal Growth" plays a key role to such planning so that each student feels that they can complete the task with some growth. When the instructional gap lacks appropriate bridging to support progress, students opt out. Supports need to be in place that helps advanced and struggling learners grow. These supports need to be respectful to the learner.

There is usually more than one way to meet student needs. Sometimes the initial approach may be more convenient to teachers, while viewed by the student as childish, stale, or boring. It is never wise to ignore the perceptions of learners, even when their view may be a misconception or lack the expertise to see the sensibleness of the option. When a learner feels ignored, they are likely to shutdown, refusing to do things the teacher's way. Better to find a third or fourth pathway with the student's help. They are more likely to invest into something that they play a part in developing.

Interests: Does the activity have meaning or value to the student? Is it worth doing?

Value can be determined in several different ways. Relate the curriculum to what the learner likes to do. A student who is interested in fishing, camping, gaming, or four wheeling is more likely to learn about research and argumentative writing if the end result is developing a video that advocates about that passion. Another student who lives or works on a dairy farm may have more interest in the sciences and math that is tied to the dairy business. A teacher's willingness to research the interests of their students, or better yet, learn from the students themselves, is more likely to engage students in substantive work.

Learning preferences: Are the tasks shaped in a way that makes sense to the student?

Teaching is a multilayered skill set because no two learners are alike. Sure, there are teaching practices that can work for groups of students. For example, consider Question and Answer sessions so they can be run for a large class, fishbowl, Socratic Seminar, or Harkness discussion. Each of these Q&A strategies approaches the experience differently. The later options include more participation than the traditional process where teachers are the center of the conversation.

Learning preferences is also about providing different ways to explore content or craft products through various forms of media and materials, from paper and pencil to sculpturing, recordings, videos, blogging, and performing—just to name a few. Some students who struggle with a math lesson may go to a site like Khan Academy to review a recording of the math concept taught in a similar fashion as the teacher. Other students may need a different site that demonstrates the math concept in a nontraditional method before understanding occurs. Considering the various ways that each learner may process information sends the message to students that they can learn content that was previously viewed as unlearnable.

The best lesson invitations by teachers that a learner can receive are learning experiences that combine some or all of the elements: readiness, interests, and/or learning preferences. Some examples include:

- Encouraging students to choose from tools that best fit how they may prefer to think through concepts (learning preferences) and using personal interests to apply the skill (interests).
- Using tiered stations where there are two or more learning tasks that students select from several options (interests) based on their current skill level (readiness).
- Having students decide on a social cause in the community that they want to support (interest). Using a range of research skills, leveled from foundational to complex (readiness), students develop a final digital product (learning preferences) to best advocate for their chosen issue.

Being intentional on incorporating readiness, interests, and learning preferences is important if students choose to accept the teacher's invitation to engage in the learning. Not everyone will do something because it is good for them. If that were the case, obesity would not be a major health issue, alcohol-related accidents would disappear, and smoking would be something remembered as a former pastime in history books.

LEARNER VOICE OVER STUDENT CHOICE

One of the basic ways that teachers can differentiate is to provide students with choices. Give them a few options from which to select how they want to do the work, topic to address, or tools to develop the product. Choice is a helpful strategy, especially when too many options can feel overwhelming to students. Options can be offered in differentiated packs based on the readiness skills of learner groups, or diversified to relate to areas of interest. The first option could be assigned based on formative assessment data. The former is presented for students to decide based on what intrigues them.

As teachers delve deeper into the layers of differentiation, looking for an expanded vision of meeting needs, offering choice alone limits a learner's voice. Consider that the choices provided are designed by the teacher. The student generally has no input in the development of the choices. Therefore, the options are based on the perspective of what the teacher thinks is inviting to students. Every learner is unique, and teachers as learners are no different. Higher levels of differentiation provide and encourage learners to insert their voice in how to grow their understanding and expertise of concepts and skills.

This idea of students taking control of their learning is not a new concept.[1] In studies on adult learning, including the learner is an essential component. For example, Learning Forward, an international organization, states in their Standards for Professional Learning:

> Educators are responsible for taking an active role in selecting and constructing learning designs that facilitate their own and others' learning. They choose appropriate learning designs to achieve their individual, team, or school goals. Educators' learning characteristics and preferences also inform decisions about learning designs.[2]

Make learning relevant and meaningful to what adult learners feel is important to their work or interests. The immediate pushback is that children are not adults. Their cognitive development is different, and their level of knowledge is vastly less than adults. Apples and oranges, right?

Students in preschool through adolescents are in a different space when it comes to cognition and content knowledge, with perhaps the exception proven by the TV show, *Are You Smarter Than a 5th Grader?*[3] There are differences that must be recognized. Kindergarteners learn about the life cycle through studying gardens, and later grades explore this phenomenon for more complex understanding, such as studying pollinators and pollination. Candy and pennies are used to teach counting. For literacy development, students decode sounds and practice sight words. In the English language, real-world experiences that are familiar to the student are attached to the learning: A is for apple, B is for bed, C is for cat, and D is for Dog. The list goes on.

Making learning relevant to young students' lives is just as necessary as for adult learners. Involving children in "hands-on" learning experiences is not just working with manipulatives. It's also involving students in the learning decisions.

Kindergarteners from a school in Texas host a farmer's market for the vegetables that they grow in their garden. At an elementary school in Sandusky City Schools in Ohio, young students convince city officials to fund a pollinator gardener as a step toward supporting the environment. In Michigan and Maine, students in early to late teens compose letters and essays to have an impact on community needs such as hunger, homelessness, and business entrepreneurs. Making learning contextual to a student's interests can only help learning.

Giving students the voice to determine learning decisions makes it possible for them to take responsibility for their learning, a belief often expressed by educators for what they want to see happen. Yet, is such a hope feasible? The major obstacle to true student voice can only be removed by educators. At many professional presentations, workshops, and coaching settings, when teachers are asked, what is the one action that teachers must be willing to do, so that student voice can flourish, they consistently respond:

Teachers Must Give Up Control

Most educators recognize that fostering student voice builds engagement and buy-in. When students are given the opportunity to express themselves and help forge their pathways to learning, they tend to flourish, such as seen within genius hour, MakerSpace, student-run EdCamp, and project-based learning.

Genius Hour

Referred to at the beginning of this chapter, Daniel Pink in his book *Drive* talks about a practice at Google called 20% time. This is where Google employees get one-fifth of their day to explore a private project to develop the idea into a possible innovation. Gmail, Google e-mail, came from this concept. In classrooms, teachers use this principle with their students. Learners explore a topic of their own interest and develop a deeper understanding. Whatever they craft, they share, usually in a presentation. According to Chris Kessler of www.geniushour.com,[4] there are three rules to follow when creating such an environment:

1. Start with a driving question.[5] This student-developed question is open-ended and calls for inquiry.
2. Requires research. Students need to investigate and learn more about their concept or idea so as to produce something new or innovative.
3. The result must be shared. For the investment in time, it's important that other students and adult audiences have the opportunity to learn about the students' work. Such sharing could lead to a breakthrough in thinking, and possibly collaborative opportunities.

Innovation Days at Ardis New Tech High School is an example for how genius hour can occur. As explained at the start of this chapter, it was a two-day school-wide event.

MakerSpace

In a Maker environment, students become innovators as they design prototypes for concepts, and then create the product. The range of such experiences might include three-dimensional printing, robotics, lego-based designs, or use of other materials. The principles of engineering design is one effective way to run and experience a MakerSpace. At Birmingham Covington School in Michigan, elementary-aged students use a variety of materials to create unique designs for physical product development and computer design. A three-dimensional printer is used for some of the work to bring the designs to life.

Student-Run EdCamp

Students identify topics and skills that they want to share with their peers. They plan and prepare materials and activities for the day of the EdCamp. Students sign up for different sessions to attend based on their interests. Teachers and guests also participate in the student sessions. Reading, writing, and communication skills are foundational to the event planning and implementation. At Serene Hills Elementary School in Lake Travis ISD, the entire fifth grade class ran their own EdCamp. After two weeks of planning, they ran the event. The experience was so well received by students and community that plans were in the works to do it again the following year.[6]

Project-Based Learning

When project-based learning is done well, students work with an authentic audience who may be a client, organization, or community with a need to be addressed. Learners are challenged with developing unique proposals, solutions, or awareness campaigns. Using ongoing reflection, constructive critiques, and development time, learners are able to deepen their content understanding.

An important result is deeper knowledge and application of required skills. Teachers create space for students to work on some tasks independently or in teams, while others meet with the teacher for personalized coaching.[7] There are many schools that practice effective project-based learning such as Kent Innovation High School in Grand Rapids, Michigan (based on the New Tech Network), the district-wide initiative at Metro Nashville Public Schools in Nashville, Tennessee (based on the Buck Institute for Education), and the High Tech High School campuses in San Diego, California.[8]

Teachers can become their own obstacle. Beth Rayl, a national consultant on innovative instructional practices stated:

> Too often in education we give students a false impression that there is only one right way to do things, which can stifle creativity and innovation. Instead, we should help them see that the world is full of possible solutions and encourage them to think in divergent ways. Human beings have an unquenchable curiosity that needs to be celebrated, encouraged, and developed rather than being set aside when one enters a classroom.

A simple and easy way to foster student voice is an adaptation of student choice. The teacher offers three choices. The first two options are designed by the teacher. They contain the academic requirements for the expected quality. The third choice is a challenge opportunity. The student gets to propose their idea for completing the academic requirements.

After listening to the proposal, the teacher may approve it, negotiate modifications, or send the student back to planning a new proposal idea. Teachers set a reasonable time limit. If the student cannot come up with an acceptable proposal by the deadline, he or she must choose from the original two options. Some students will prefer the teacher-designed choices. That's fine. The third option gives students the opportunity to take charge of their learning if that is their desire.

Bridging Content Understanding through Readiness Skills

Each of these implementation designs empowers student voice, which is developed through the teaching and coaching of college and career readiness skills. The application of learning and innovation skills,[9] such as communication, collaboration, problem solving, and innovation puts academia into a real-world context. This helps the learner to move from struggling with content as abstract and disconnected. They move toward understanding content as a concrete framework within the scope of real-world application.

The differentiation elements of readiness, interests, and learning preferences play an important role. Learners who actively use the learning and innovation skills are able to advocate for themselves by using networks, such as teachers and other students for assistance and resources. Students can advocate for their own differentiation needs by becoming independent learners and self-directed. These skills require coaching and monitoring by the teacher. It also requires students to have real opportunities for leading their learning, which happens only when teachers relinquish control.

LETTING GO OF CONTROL

Giving up control is difficult for teachers because of the pressure that they feel from mandates by their school, district, and possibly state or country. While these pressures are real, they are adult issues, usually not of primary importance for learners. For students to have a meaningful voice in their learning, teachers must willingly cede control.

Teachers must trust in the intellectual capacity and powerful drive that exists within learners to acquire and practice skills needed or required for academic understandings. The doubtful may look to genius hour, Montessori programs, design thinking, or a constructivist learning experience. If these systems for learning do not convince some, then they should look within themselves: What motivates their desire to learn something? Is it when they are told everything, or when they find the work relevant to their personal needs? It is better to lead self-discovery, then to be told what to think.

Letting go of control does not mean stepping away from teaching. It means stepping out of the way of the learner's path so that they can journey alongside or ahead of the teacher. Teachers develop the framework within which students can flourish with their ideas for how to learn and what to explore. Students are encouraged to ask questions that lead them to deeper questions. When teachers have a firm understanding of the skills and concepts that must be developed, they can provide effective coaching and guidance on the learner experience that is personalized.

The movement toward such experiences, like genius hour and Maker-Space, gains support as ways for students to drive their learning. In Eastern Carver County Schools, in Chaska, Minnesota, students at Chanhassen High School collaborate with teachers on their learning.[10] Learners can spend part or all of their class time in spaces that are setup as independent study, collaboration spaces, and coaching support by a teacher on duty.

Staff and students recognize that the classroom is not always the learning space needed at particular moments in the curriculum. An advanced student may need individual or small group coaching that sparks a solo inquiry experience. A struggling learner may need a workshop on a specific skill or concept, and then practice alone or with others in the collaboration space. Initiatives such as this represent how educators are recognizing the value of including students as active consumers of their learning.

Truly empowering students with their learning frees up teachers to have a greater impact on more learners then occurs in a traditional setting. Students will become active learners, rather than passive receivers of instruction. Coaching is necessary, as the opportunities provided may be their first experience of true voice. Using a gradual release approach, all students can rise to the challenge of higher expectations.

ELIMINATING AIRPLANE MODE
IN EDUCATION—PART TWO

Trusting in student capacity to rise to the learning outcomes or high standards may seem overwhelming. Such level of differentiation requires some level of risk taking by educators who must believe that they are not "the" source of expertise and knowledge. Such thinking leads to the airplane mode, as addressed in Chapter 3.[11]

Students experience the airplane mode in two ways, one less so than the other. The first way occurs in schools that limit or attempt to ban student access to their own electronic devices while in school. The reasons vary for the limited access to technology, but the result is the same: students have limited access to the tools and resources that could help them succeed based on their readiness, interests, and learning preferences. Teachers are also limited by the various means that they can provide quality learning experiences that meet the needs of all of their students.

Fortunately, the number of schools who limit or place bans on such devices appears to be decreasing. With initiatives like one-to-one devices and BYOD (Bring Your Own Device), such self-inflicted wound to learning is fading.

The second way is of greater concern and still quite pervasive in most schools. Today, students have greater influence on the world than ever before through social media and their networks. For example, many students of elementary and secondary school age consume content on such sites as YouTube, Facebook, Instagram, and Twitter, to name just a few. As new tools are introduced, these learners are migrating to different avenues for communication.

A large number of these students create content. They comment on discussion boards and chat sessions via such tools as Skype and mobile apps. Many create music and videos, which are published online. YouTubers is one example of entrepreneurs, many are preteens and teens, who earn an income from publishing content on YouTube. Through YouTube channels and other social media portals like Instagram, youths are generating a following of viewers that may range from the thousands to the millions. There are many such sites that range from twenty-five to hundreds of followers.

The questions for educators are:

- How many of your students have a following, who are potentially influenced by them?
- How many of your students create and publish content?
- How many generate revenue from their efforts?
- How often have you incorporated such talent and experiences into the curriculum work?

For most of these students, their teachers have little knowledge or understanding of what they do via social media, or the followers they influence. When these students leave school each day, they are no longer cut off from the world that matters most to them because of their followers who value their efforts. When teachers know and collaborate with these students through their sphere of influence, stronger contexts can be made to curriculum and student engagement rises through the value placed on their own life experiences.

End the airplane mode syndrome for greater student buy-in to the learning.

TEACHER GROWTH MIND-SET LEADS TO LEARNER VOICE

If empowering and nurturing learner voices is so important, and generally accepted by teachers as necessary for lifelong learning, why does it not already happen building wide? The lack of the obvious for learner voice has many reasons, something for which an entire book could be committed to the need. Carol Dweck's work[12] on Growth versus Fixed Mindset is one path to take for understanding why learner voice in many schools is limited to nonexistent.

A growth mind-set believes that anyone can learn and grow skills with hard work and dedication. There is no guarantee that each person will grow to similar heights, but a teacher with such a mind-set works diligently through differentiation so all can learn. Educators with a fixed mind-set say all students can learn, but then list all of the obstacles that prevent them from ensuring learner success.

They are mired in frustration, or for some in relief, with what they feel is beyond their control—district mandates, state or national standards, lack of parental support at home or school, poverty, limited resources, large class size, not enough instructional time, and too much curriculum to cover. The list of rationalizations can be an endless spiral that distracts competent teachers with the best of intentions from doing what must be done so that all learners under their charge learn.

Teachers with a growth mind-set about their craft and their charges tackle the many obstacles through what they have the greatest influence—their expertise, craft, and understanding of students with whom they have direct contact. Educators with a fixed mind-set retreat to defensive bunkers where they believe they must rely on themselves to find answers. This results in such teachers trying to control everything, and trusting and relying only on themselves.

Meanwhile, educators with a growth mind-set realize that to overcome the many obstacles, they must trust in the capacity of their greatest resource— the learners under their charge. Tapping the rich sources of intellectual and creative thinking of the students via their readiness, interests, and learning preferences can lead to truly innovative approaches to teaching and learning experiences.

In the ideal situation, the leadership involves teachers in such experiences demonstrating a release of control. Through risk taking and reflection on practice, teachers do the same with their students. For some educators, the real-world situation is that such approaches are grown in individual classrooms until the branches extend throughout the school as common practice. Even when the process drags and buds wither along some branches, a teacher who gardens her own classroom can establish firm roots in the students he or she influences.

CREATING A CULTURE FOR STUDENT VOICE

"Do as I say, not as I do" is an adage that is sometimes used for instructing others about the conflicting messages sent about what is important. For student voice, a teacher must be mindful of the ramifications of what they communicate to students in their daily interactions. With the best of intentions or

in idle jests, words can send messages that have unintended negative consequences on student lives.

If one believes that all students can achieve, differentiation provides multiple paths for students to make learning real for themselves. For example, a
teacher might tier instruction so that students needing more basics on reading
practices and students who are ready for advanced instructional-level reading
get their needs met, while at the same time conducting important research
for a persuasive presentation about issues such as renewable energy, recy-
cling, global warming, or homelessness. But if a teacher gives the advanced
students the task of proposing renewable energy options for the community,
and assigns the students needing basic reading practices with producing a
brochure on the facts, a disturbing message is sent to all students about limits
of intellectual capacity.

In *Creating Cultures of Thinking*, Ron Ritchhart[13] shares many examples
of the importance of teachers' actions and words that either empower student
learning or disenfranchise their voice. When students are engaged in work
that is valued by others or a community, they are more willing to put forth the
effort needed. Students will need structures and supports that address gaps in
their understanding or confidence in doing the work.

The students include advanced learners as well as the others. If an
advanced learner is not asking questions or struggling with key parts of the
instruction, then they are likely not growing. Providing such scaffolds helps
all learners meet or exceed expectations. Messages of "how can we generate
ideas or answers to this problem" and "what do you think would be the best
way to express these ideas" send the message "you are capable of this work."

PEDAGOGICAL NEEDS FOR STUDENT VOICE

Empowering students to own their learning experience may require a shift
in how one thinks about the purpose and outcomes for education. Rethink-
ing is needed regarding the roles and responsibilities of educators and their
students, along with the impact and effect of curriculum. Carol Tomlinson,
in her book, *Fulfilling the Promise of the Differentiated Classroom*, writes
extensively about this important relationship of students, teachers, and curriculum, which is well worth reading. For purposes here, let's consider what
teachers can influence and control: their own thinking.

1. Prioritize the Belief in Students' Capacity for Learning

Many schools and districts have in their vision or mission statement an idea
that essentially states a belief that "all students can learn." The idea is one

filled with hope and promise. Yet in practice, there are many feelings of frustration at real and perceived obstacles that appear to following through on such an idea. For example, if time is limited, how is it possible to ensure that all learners are growing? The answer is to place learner needs first.

Stephen Covey called this habit: put first things first.[14] If student learning is the priority, then differentiation becomes essential for such success. Saying what students "can't do" or "won't do" should encourage teachers to reflect on what they "are doing," and how they could transform their practice so that students do what is needed of them. When people struggle with learning and feel the weight of frustration, they may respond from a fight or flight perspective.

Through differentiation, a teacher can help learners to keep fighting up the tunnel toward daylight. When people believe that they already know the content being taught, some will choose to demand more challenge, while others will quietly pass the time thinking thoughts that are far away from the dull experience at hand. Through differentiation, a teacher can provide the advanced learner with the appropriate challenge that keeps their mind busy with growing dendrites.

Learners of any age will respond in similar ways regardless of age or level of content expertise. Belief in their capacity to learn requires that educators believe in their own capacity to grow their practice to meet the diverse needs of their students. What better way is there for educators to practice lifelong learning in their profession?

2. Be an Active Learner

Anyone who believes or says that teaching is easy is naive at best. Learning is essential to life. For the health of any society, this is as deep a responsibility for educators as it is for the medical profession. The quality and quantity of those educated can significantly affect all facets of culture and society for communities and nations. Student voice has simple steps to start, as shared in this chapter, but also has complexity and nuances that require high expertise in one's profession and the ability to adapt and change one's own thinking through a growth mind-set.

Educators must learn continuously about tools and pedagogical approaches. Explore how to adapt them for meeting learner needs. This is what separates the good teachers from the mediocre. Good teachers are willing to try new ideas. They want students to succeed and are open to ideas when presented to them or found in articles and books. They find ways to model their thinking to students, to show that learning can be difficult for teachers too.

The exceptional educators are those who, despite fears of failure or reprisals by leadership or colleagues, try new and different approaches to learning experiences to ignite and feed student voice. These teachers use data from various sources, including the students, to create learning opportunities. They use a feedback loop with students to listen and learn from them about the successes and failures of the lesson. Negative experiences are simply fuel for the next experiment. Such teachers are not necessarily fearless nor ignore the weight of pressure to maintain the status quo. They find ways to move forward because of the positive growth they see in their students.

3. Reflect on Practice

Teach in the way that students need, not in the way that is always comfortable for one's instructional delivery. This was discussed in a different chapter regarding the formative assessment cycle. When student learning is the priority over all other mandates and expectations, teachers can find the liberation to do what is needed by their students. The key is for teachers to begin with effecting what they can influence: themselves.

Student voice is scary on the surface when one does not know how to approach it. Start by being honest with oneself about the preferred teaching practices of choice. Teachers tend to use the instructional strategies that suit themselves. When those approaches do not work for a group of students, the response can erroneously be to blame the students' motivation. Yes, student engagement does impact leaning. The questions to ask are:

- How could I provide this instruction differently?
- What would the students say they would prefer as a means to tackle the work?
- What would parents say are their child's school history of learning strengths and anxieties?
- What is outside my comfort zone and how can I overcome it for the sake of my students?

The last question is important for recognizing that sometimes what limits the students' progress is not their motivation but that of the instructor's wiliness to move beyond his or her own comfort zone. The power of self-reflection can have a tremendous and positive impact on both the learning of students and the teacher who supports them.

4. Communicate and Involve Parents

A parent shared his concerns when his daughter entered a new school. She was an active student who completed assignments and had success in most subject areas. Math was a source of anxiety for her and her parents. Her experience with learning math was mixed. Some teachers used differentiation to get to understand her strengths and areas of need, and crafted learning experiences where she gained understanding and confidence.

The father shared that unfortunately many of his daughter's math teachers seemed either overwhelmed with the number of learners needing help or chose staying on a curriculum pace over reteaching based on learner needs, such as connecting the abstract math concepts with concrete real-world examples that students could apply. His daughter has had several tutors throughout her school career. All were picked based on their expert level of using multiple data sources to apply the differentiation lens.

The father hoped for a better outcome at the new school. He and his wife composed an e-mail for the teacher, sharing about their daughter's strengths, confidence needs, and other insights based her school math history.

Parents and guardians tend to know much about their children that can be helpful to teachers. Using surveys can collect immediate data at the beginning of the year. Another tool is to provide written updates about the students at timely opportunities as needed. Knowing the parents need for information can be important for having their active support at home and in the classroom.

Syndee Malek[15] shares this experience when she was an elementary school principal regarding parents:

> One practice that I used to have as a teacher was to have the parents write a letter to me telling me about their child. . . . The insides of how they learned, what their strengths or weaknesses are. . . . It gave me an opportunity to know them from the parents point of view. I think the parents loved writing a letter to me as much as I loved receiving them. . . . And I always ask the parent to have that with their child when school started. It helped create a picture in my mind of who that child was. For me it helped build relationships with the family.

It is important to keep a pulse on knowing about students from themselves and their parents or guardians. A result is that teachers can use the current data to craft or cocreate with their learners a lesson experience that students will opt in.

5. Give Up Control

This idea has been discussed extensively in this chapter and is mentioned here as an important reminder. Students who do not perform to expectations need more opportunities to practice the skills and experience it through new perspectives, such as include students in co-constructing the learning experience. When students do not reach expectations—that is shared failure. How the teachers choose to own their responsibility starts the first steps toward students accepting accountability.

Control that leads to teacher-centered instruction meets employee needs, not the needs of all their students. An example occurs often in the tried-and-true strategy of teacher-led questions and answers. Sit in any classroom, and see a typical act play itself out.

The teacher leads with a question. He or she may wait for an answer or use name sticks to call on a random student. In either case, the student attempts an answer. The teacher might respond with approval and/or add clarifications to the student response. This ritual is repeated until all teacher-planned questions are shared.

In the best scenario, the teacher and the called-on students have a good back and forth of asking and answering questions. The student passivity may not be as apparent to the trained eye, unless you were to contrast this Q&A experience with ones that used such protocols as Socratic Seminar, Three Levels of Text, Save the Last Word, and the Harkness or Spider Discussion.[16] In each case, the students lead the discussion. They ask questions that lead to more questions as they collectively explore content.

"But those protocols will take more time" some would say, and in most cases that may be true. What is also clear is that all students are engaged in the exploration of content and learning outcomes. All students are supported by their peers during the protocols. Most important, all students are encouraged and supported within the respective protocol structures to have an active voice that leads to deeper understanding then a teacher-led discussion.

PRACTICAL SUPPORT OF STUDENT VOICE

Where pedagogy is the mind-set and guide for thoughtful practices, how does one put ideals into concrete action? Here are active steps for bringing to life student voice for effective differentiation.

1. Informed Decision Making

Students can generate ideas in an open-ended session. This approach can scare many teachers as they wonder how to align the curriculum outcomes that students must demonstrate achievement.

A starting point is for teachers to own the framework. Give students guidance and structures within which students propose and decide their learning paths. What are the skills that must be demonstrated? What are the nonnegotiables, both academic and logistical, that students must include in their approach? The framework can be a detailed structure with specific steps or sections that students can customize to their preferences.

Another approach is to give students an open-ended space to design their approach to the work, while using checklists of required learning outcomes. Within this range, there may be discussions or negotiations about the make-up of the work. Give into the students' ideas as much as is reasonably possible. The more that they get their way, the more responsibility that they assume for the work.

A second consideration is to make clear how the required skills will be assessed. When students understand these expectations, they can use rubrics and qualitative checklists as an effective guide for developing and revising their products. Never assume that students understand the assessment process from one review of the tool. Better understanding leads to clearer conversations for students to propose alternative ways to demonstrate learning.

2. Conduct Coaching Conversations with Students

True student voice requires ongoing conversations about the work and how students could tackle expectations. Expect that some or many students will struggle with finding their voice. This is often due to the education environment enculturing students to be passive learners, awaiting assignments to be given to them.

Coaching students to develop their voice are also opportunities for thoughtful learning conversations. Here are important coaching steps to develop a teacher's communication toolkit.

Step One: Pause and Paraphrase

Listen to students' ideas and thoughts. Before asking any questions, pause to digest their thinking, and then paraphrase what the student said. This action of pausing and paraphrasing models listening skills. The pause demonstrates active digestion of the person's words. Paraphrasing checks for mutual understanding. If the paraphrasing is inaccurate, the student will say so, and re-explain. If the paraphrasing is accurate, the students may say more to add to their narrative.

Step Two: Follow a Paraphrase with a Clarifying Question

Sometimes a student will not share enough information, or may not know what to add or elaborate. In this instance, the teacher follows a paraphrase, to show he or she is listening, with a clarifying question. The intent is to help the student mine new ideas or unpack what they have already shared. The intent of such questions is to get more information.

Step Three: Follow a Paraphrase with a Probing Question

Show understanding with a paraphrase, and then follow up with a probing question. Such a question occurs when the student is ready to uncover an idea or direction for their work. The intent is to support the student's thinking on how they wish to proceed. It is important not to direct students to a teacher's idea. Such Jedi Mind-tricks[17] creates distrust that will be difficult and time-consuming to repair.

When done well, probing questions inspire students to ideas that they uncovered with the teacher's help. This can lead to stronger buy-in by the student. Once the idea is established, the teacher may switch from coaching to negotiator so that the final experience will satisfy learning outcomes, while remaining the student's idea intact.

3. Grow Students into Active Learners

The education system tends to develop passive learners. Students who resist taking a lead may do so because they are comfortable with the existing system learned over the years, or because they have had little opportunity to develop the needed skills to lead their learning. People can be creatures of habit. Years of being part of an institution that demands sitting quietly for attendance and instructional delivery takes its toll. Classroom management that follows the simple and direct approach of maintaining control reinforces the message that to succeed means to follow the lead of the teacher.

Managing a large number of students is an important skill set. Teachers who cannot gain the attention of their students are in danger of not being able to provide any effective learning experiences. With this understanding, it is possible to manage a classroom that is conducive to learning and has students being active in the learning process.

A teacher must know their comfort zone, as discussed previously, and find the area to start giving students opportunity to lead. Often at first, such experiences will require coaching along with a gradual release process. This may start with choices in activities that slowly include limited voice. As the culture develops, add more student voice. The results can be quite positive.

FINAL THOUGHTS

Student Voice is an active part of differentiation. When students are involved in their learning in ways that are meaningful and respectful to them, they can more efficiently get their needs met. When teachers control all aspects of the learning experience, they are essentially implementing a setting that suits only a portion of their students. Voice is a way to get real insight into needs by gaining the students' perspective.

A big fear with empowering Student Voice is the perceived loss of control. One could argue that such control is illusionary. Just listen to a teacher's complaints about students not doing work at a high-quality level, or not participating in lesson activities. These concerns or complaints go to the heart of how students respond to teacher-developed lessons through the lens of readiness, interests, and learning preferences.

If students do not see connections or supports that are positive, within those lenses, they may likely disengage. When teachers use such data to plan crossroad lessons, more students are able to find learning connections at an appropriate level of support.

Keep in mind that to change practice requires an openness to self-reflect on instructional practices with a growth mind-set. Use the ideas and suggestions in this chapter to launch or further refine Student Voice in your sphere of influence.

INVITATIONS TO REFLECTION

As a result of this chapter, use the lens for differentiation to consider the following questions for a self-guided exploration of your practice and those whom you support.

1. Which are two of the biggest fears about including more student voice? What might be the reasons for such fears, and what could be helpful responses to them?
2. What are ways that you use choice to support learners? How might adding more voice over choice impact your work and that of those you teach or lead?
3. Relinquishing control can be challenging. What are the pros and cons for teachers maintaining sole control of the learning and environment? What are the pros and cons for sharing control with students? How might the cons be managed to foster student voice?
4. In the section, "Pedagogical Needs for Student Voice," what idea was affirmational to your thinking and practice? Share why. What idea might you find challenging to either change your practice or that of others? Share why.
5. In the section, "Practical Supports for Student Voice," what step would you spend more time further developing? Why is that step important for those you work with?
6. As a result of the ideas about Student Voice in this chapter, how could you be an ambassador for student voice in your school or organization? Why might such actions be worth doing?

Crossroad Planning Invitation

• Design a learning experience that promotes student voice. Consider using the implementation frames discussed in this chapter.

Facilitate a group or staff dialogue about student voice. Use the implementation frames discussed in this chapter. Consider practicing the pause and paraphrase as addressed under Conduct Coaching Conversations with Students.

Enrichment Option

Make a list of three steps that you will take to increase student voice using the five steps for "Practical Support of Student Voice."

NOTES

1. There are a range of educational programs and pedagogy that promote some degree of student-led learning: Montessori, Reggio Emilia, and Constructivist philosophy. Some curriculum structures support student voice when it intentionally becomes the focus: project-based learning, place-based learning, inquiry-based learning, authentic learning experiences, and the use of 21st-century skills. Find more information at www.SoAllCanLearn.org.

2. Learning Forward on Standards for Professional Learning. https://learningforward.org/standards/learning-designs. The Pew Research Center did a survey of adults: Lifelong Learning and Technology by John Horrigan (March 22, 2016). The responses were interesting in that personalized voice was prevalent. http://www.pewinternet.org/2016/03/22/lifelong-learning-and-technology/.

3. *Are You Smarter Than a 5th Grader* was a game show where adult contestants answer questions found in textbooks for 5th graders. A panel of 5th-grade students tries to help contestants.

4. Chris Kesler. "What Is Genius Hour?—Introduction to Genius Hour in the Classroom," https://www.youtube.com/watch?v=NMFQUtHsWhc, September 6, 2013.

5. For more information about Driving Questions, article links can be found at www.OpeningPaths.org or www.SoAllCanLearn.org.

6. More details about this event are shared in Chapter 9 regarding differentiation through interests.

7. Research that shows one important connection to project-based learning and differentiation is *Inclusion and Problem-Based Learning: Roles of Students in a Mixed-Ability Group* by Brian R. Belland, Krista D. Glazewski, and Peggy A. Ertmer. https://www.amle.org/BrowsebyTopic/WhatsNew/WNDet/TabId/270/ArtMID/888/ArticleID/66/Inclusion-and-Problem-Based-Learning-Roles-of-Students-in-a-Mixed-Ability-Group.aspx or read the full document at: https://www.amle.org/portals/0/pdf/rmle/rmle_vol32_no9.pdf.

Find additional research at the Buck Institute for Education. http://www.bie.org/ or http://www.bie.org/objects/cat/research.

8. The New Tech Network: http://newtechnetwork.org/, Buck Institute for Education: http://www.bie.org/, High Tech High: http://www.hightechhigh.org/, Expeditionary Learning: http://eleducation.org/.

9. P21's Learning and Innovation Skills are important for connecting curriculum to real-world applications. http://www.p21.org/about-us/p21-framework.

10. Chanhassen High School exploration of personalization is part of a larger initiative by the district for seeking better means to meet needs of all learners. Learn more about the district's vision and efforts at: http://wearepersonalizedlearning.org/.

11. Airplane Mode: When boarding a commercial airplane, one of the directions given before takeoff is that all cellular devices must be turned off. Internet access is provided once the plane takes off (as a fee as of this writing) by the operators of the plane. For most passengers, they are cut off from the rest of the world during the time of their flight. When the plane has landed, one of the announcements made is that cellular devices can be turned on. Often, passengers do not wait for the announcement as indicated by the many buzzes and ringtones during the landing. The sounds of the phones indicate all the messages that were in queue during the flight are now delivered to the passengers.

12. Carol S. Dweck. *Mindset: The New Psychology of Success—How We Can Learn to Fulfill Our Potential.* Random House. February 28, 2006.

13. Ron Ritchhart. *Creating Cultures of Thinking: The 8 Forces We Must Master to Truly Transform Our Schools.* Jossey-Bass. March 9, 2015.

14. Stephen Covey. *Seven Habits of Highly Effective People.* Free Press. 1989.

15. Syndee Malek is currently a school improvement consultant in the largest county in Michigan. A teacher, former principal, and district administrator, she is widely respected for her leadership work with administrators and aspiring teachers as leaders.

16. These protocols are discussed in the later chapters on applying differentiation through content, process, and product based on students' readiness, interests, and learning preferences. Here is an article that provides one perspective on their use:

John McCarthy. *Establishing a Culture of Student Voice.* http://www.edutopia.org/blog/establishing-culture-of-student-voice-john-mccarthy.

17. In the original *Star Wars*, Jedi Mind-Tricks were used by Jedi's to mentally manipulate others to do their bidding. This term is used in coaching when someone tries to impose their ideas as if it were those of the coached individuals.

Chapter 7

Differentiation in Practice: Readiness for *All*

Authentic assessments that are truly connected to real-world relevance naturally lend themselves to differentiation. Through authentic learning experiences, students have the freedom to determine their path to create a value-added solution to a challenge, as there is no one right answer. An authentic learning experience, and thus the assessment of it, provides the opportunity to meet each student where they are and to scaffold throughout, as needed. As each student may create a different solution, each student creates their own opportunity to allow you, the teacher, to differentiate for them.

—Dayna Laur, national consultant and author[1]

One certainty in education is that with every group of learners, the level of understanding and skills will vary. Diversity exists even when students are grouped for gifted, honors, advanced placement, remedial, and especially special education. A portion of students are easy to identify. Students identified through tests as gifted and those in need of IEPs or moderate support for learning disabilities. The difficult ones to identify are strong in some areas and struggle with comprehension in some areas. This can be found in any group of students regardless if the class is remedial or an advanced placement course.

The only place where differences in learning might not exist is where information downloads are done for a group of robots (although the quality of circuits and engineered connections could vary by the different people and machines that manufactured the parts that make the whole).

The diversity of learners is both a blessing and a challenge. "How do I meet the diverse needs of my students within the program I teach?" is the question often asked. The short answer is to start wherever the students are.

Readiness and assessments for learning are tightly wound together as an interdependent weave. Readiness without assessments is like attempting a penalty kick in soccer, blindfolded, guided on to a field, without any sense of where on the field you stand. The goal might be in front, behind, or to the side, and be half a pitch away. A lack of understanding what the learner needs may often lead to false or wasteful remedies.

Assessments for learning without readiness are like looking at sports data for its own sake, and not for improving the athlete and team. Data collected and analyzed can inform teachers of the needs for each of their students. If the teacher continues with instruction that is not adapted or reshaped based on the data, the time on assessments is wasted.

Assessments for learning inform a teacher of what a student needs to succeed. If a teacher chooses not to follow through, that is akin to a doctor who identifies the root cause of an illness or wound, but withholds the remedy. Both cases are professional malpractice.

Acting with the best remedies for learning also sends a message to students that they matter. Their needs are important enough to be incorporated into the learning experiences, including appropriate supports so that they can learn and grow. Such messages can go a long way toward convincing students to buy-in and work with teachers around curriculum expectations.

READINESS GUIDELINES

What follows is a look at characteristics of readiness—how students enter learning experiences—through the lenses of content, processes, and products—how teachers frame and plan instruction. Different strategies and approaches will be used as examples to reflect on the identified readiness characteristic.

One important context for readiness planning across content, processes, and products is to plan with the end in mind (Wiggins and McTighe).[2] Here is a set of guidelines when planning differentiation through readiness:

1. Be clear on the learning outcomes;
2. Create a draft of the post assessment for the outcomes;
3. Draft the initial learning experience;
4. Review student assessment data for adaptations, personalization, or tiering;
5. Revise the learning experience and post assessment;
6. Implement and reflect following the formative assessment cycle (FAC).

Any high-quality instructional strategy or program can be differentiated to the needs of learners. In this table, the examples are a small portion of the expansive list that could be generated. Use these examples as an opportunity for reflective dialogue about how to adapt the characteristics used into other strategies and programs used in your school or classroom.

Table 7.1.   Readiness-Based Examples

Learners are motivated or self-determine action by how learning experiences are structured. They are likely to participate when one or more of these areas are met: readiness, interests, and/or learning preferences.	**Readiness** Structure learning from: • Part to whole: segment into parts to digest • Simple to complex • Dependence to interdependence
Content How is access to information made for learners? How are learners able to access and understand the concepts and skills?	• Tiered activities at needed levels • Leveled reading/cognitive materials • Graphic organizer: help see content in segments • Centers: Assign content and directions based on skill level • Learning contracts • Mini-lessons • "Say Something" or "Last Word" for readings • Enrichments/extensions
Process How can learners digest content and make into their own?	• Tiered activities at needed levels • Centers: Provide skill-appropriate tasks for each group of learners • Think Dots/Task Cards • Menus • Think-Tac-Toe • Enrichments/extensions • Project/problem-based learning • Writer's workshop • 6 traits • Web quest
Product How would learners distill what they learned by application, demonstration, or performance?	• Tiered and addresses same outcomes • Project/problem-based learning • RAFTS: Options are simple to complex • Think Dots/Task Cards • Rubric-based activities • Design something • Performance task • Enrichments/extensions

TEACHING READINESS THROUGH CONTENT

Content differentiated by readiness helps students acquire the understanding they need to lay foundations for later learning. Without readiness, the teaching approach tends to be a one size fits all. The result is a failure in student achievement and a widening of the learning gap. There is also a failure by the teacher to find the approach that best helps students learn what they need to know. When readiness is a factor in planning, students make more connections and build confidence. The teachers may find that they need to do less reteaching because of the well laid out supports, differentiated to the needs of each learner.

Example One: Portioning Content

Martin Diller is a 40+ year veteran teacher at Estrella Foothills High School in Goodyear, Arizona. He starts every American Government and Economics class with a news video. He uses each episode as a connection to the learning outcomes for that day's lesson. The news show reports on events from around the globe and domestically in the United States. Four to six topics are usually addressed during the 10 to 15-minute video.

When shown without breaks, many of the students could not recall nor discuss the topics. Martin Diller made a few simple changes that transformed the learning experience. The tables were reconfigured from rows into clusters, where six students sat. Each cluster elected a president who became the lead spokesperson for their group. Martin Diller used an online tool, EdPuzzle,[3] which pauses the video at chosen points, usually every three to five minutes and displays questions generated by the teacher. Students discuss the questions in their table groups. Martin Diller randomly calls on a president to either answer the question or to choose one of his or her table group to respond.

Analysis and Reflection

In this example, differentiation through readiness is addressed through a combination of tools. Serving content in digestible sections is an important feature. When there is much to be introduced, direct instruction is a common tool. While much content can be given out, there is no guarantee that all students will take in all of the salient details. Dividing content into portions enables learners to focus on the parts that later make up the whole.

In the social studies example, the news video is paused at specific points so that students can answer questions that make clear knowledge, and later reflect on the implications from the events. Later pauses can include some questions that increase with complexity based on the collective knowledge reviewed during the progress of the video, or other sources like articles and chapters.

Dividing content into portions is supported by the management strategy of placing students into table teams. Group dialogue about the questions can provide individual support. Listening to different answers helps learners to build clarity. Disagreement and consensus both serve as important ways to develop understanding and inquiry questions. The quiet ones must pay attention to the conversation. They are usually internal thinkers[4] who process their thoughts internally to cement their knowledge. This active silent thinking is as valuable as for those who prefer dialogue. All of the students need to participate because any one of them might be called upon by the table president to speak for the group.

The key to portioning content is to be clear on the learning outcomes.

1. What are the key concepts and understandings that learners need to take away from the content?

   In the example, the outcomes varied such as understanding the role of the press in relation to the First Amendment to the Constitution or the impact of global events on U.S. foreign policy.

2. What will students need to do to achieve the outcomes?

   Students answered question prompts that the teacher embedded in the video at strategic points. He also used groups as study support teams to reflect and discuss about possible answers to the prompts, before having randomly selected teams report their ideas.

3. How will students show understanding of the content?

   The teacher had table teams report their answers. Sometimes the response leads to follow-up questions that other students answered. When a student appeared to struggle with an answer, teammates were encouraged to support. Sometimes other teams contributed their thoughts. The responses informed the teacher of the trend for understanding existed.

4. Did all students or some have a clear understanding?

   As a result of the student responses, the teacher was able to do some initial formative assessment on how the students progressed. The participation and answers informed as to areas that needed more clarification and which students were ready to tackle more academically complex questions.

Example Two: Tiering Content

This assignment about voice, one of the 6+ writing traits is to help learners understand how voice is used in writing. Think Dot was the format used for this activity. There are six boxes. Each contains a task that addresses the concept, parts, and functions of fractions, in different ways. Students worked in teams to complete the tasks by rolling a die, or using a digital version. The results from 1 to 6 indicated which box to work on. This engaging activity has students randomly selecting the order of when tasks get completed.

The teacher used the tiering strategy for meeting readiness needs. There were two versions of the assignment, both addressing the same learning outcomes. A tiered activity may include two or more versions of the activity to meet the academic learning outcomes. Students were grouped by shared level for academic support. Look at the two versions and identify the differences, and which Think Dot has more complexity.

Think Dots

Learning Objective: Understand how authors use voice to create interesting writing or communication.
Evidence/Assessment: 5 minute free-write describing their understanding of Author's Voice.

Tiered: At-Target Level

Instructions: In your groups discuss each of the tasks and possible answers. Next, divide up the work so that each person has 2 tasks. Complete your assigned tasks individually. You may ask for help. The work must be in your own words.

Highlight and discuss 3 words or phrases that show Junie B. Jones' personality in her voice (example is in bold): "Dear people who are reading this, Hurray! Hurray! I am so glad you found my Web site! See my picture on the front of this screen? I am the star of this **whole entire** page, I tell you! There are lots of fun things to do at this place! Like yesterday I colored on the coloring pages and I didn't even follow the coloring rules! 'Cause I colored my face green. And I colored the grass blue. And I colored the sky pink. And the world looked very beautiful that way!" (• one dot)	Which demonstrates a stronger voice? Explain 2–3 differences in a T chart. 1. The wolf is a serial killer who almost claimed 2 more lives. He broke into Granny's house, taking her by surprise. He laid a trap for Red by impersonating her Granny. That was sick because he was playing with Red's emotions, like her life was his toy. Red figured out his game, acted fast with the cell phone, and got help from the neighbor. 2. The wolf is the antagonist of the story. He is very scary because he tried to eat the grandmother and Red. Breaking into Granny's house and chasing Red showed how the wolf was dangerous. In the end, granny and Red were saved by the neighbor who arrived just in time. (• one dot)	Say the following statement 3 times. Choose a different emotion to say the statement. **"Ew, is that really a wolf?"** • Neutral • Fear • Sarcastic • Happy or Loving • Anger or Hate • Sadness Identify which character tag best fits how you said the statement: 1. Her voice trembled and tears rimmed her eyes. 2. She squealed and bounded like a bunny. 3. She said like a robot. 4. She said, holding her nose. 5. She bowed her head, and shuddered. 6. The words forced through her teeth into a growl. (••• three dots)
3. Word Choice: Describe how much you like your favorite fruit (ex. Apple). Do not use the words: like, love, best, good, favorite, or wonderful. (•• two dots)	List 3 songs. For each describe the emotion or tone of voice. For example: "Happy Birthday to You" – Joyful and full of excitement. (••• three dots)	Word Choice: Draw a scene from a story or your own life. Use colors to represent the mood. (••• three dots)

*Set up activity: Students wrote their meaning of voice and shared in a class discussion.

Figure 7.1. Example: Tiered Version One. Former excerpt from http://www.randomhouse.com/kids/junieb/letter/letter.html

Think Dots

Learning Objective: Understand how authors use voice to create interesting writing or communication.
Evidence/Assessment: 5 minute free-write describing their understanding of Author's Voice.

Tiered: Targeted Outcome for Advanced Learners

Instructions: In your groups discuss each of the tasks and possible answers. Next, divide up the work so that each person has 2 tasks. Complete your assigned tasks individually. You may ask for help. The work must be in your own words.

Review the 6 Traits rubric for Voice and Word Choice. Explain the characteristics that gives this letter strong voice:
 	
"Dear people who are reading this, Hurray! Hurray! I am so glad you found my Web site! See my picture on the front of this screen? I am the star of this whole entire page, I tell you!
   There are lots of fun things to do at this place! Like yesterday I colored on the coloring pages and I didn't even follow the coloring rules! 'Cause I colored my face green. And I colored the grass blue. And I colored the sky pink. And the world looked very beautiful that way!"
(Junie B. Jones)
 	
●
	Which demonstrates a stronger voice? List at least 2 differences and 2 similarities using a Venn Diagram.
	1. The wolf is a serial killer who almost claimed 2 more lives. He broke into Granny's house, taking her by surprise. He laid a trap for Red by impersonating her Granny. That was sick because he was playing with Red's emotions, like her life was his toy. Red figured out his game, acted fast with the cell phone, and got help from the neighbor.
	2. 911! Help me! A wolf is chasing me in my grandmother's house. He followed me or somehow got to my granny's house ahead of me. I found him in her bed, wearing her nightgown. Oh, granny where are you? Police please hurry. Wait, that's the neighbor's voice. I'm in the basement. Help. That smell, like a hot wind against my face. Oh, what big teeth you have. Eek! Click.
	●
		Say the following statement 3 times. Choose a different emotion to say the statement.
		
		"Ew, is that really a wolf?"
		
		• Neutral • Fear
		• Sarcastic • Happy or
		• Anger or Loving
		   Hate • Sadness
		
		Then, add a character tag that _shows_ the voice.
		
		●●●

Describe your favorite fruit as if you hate it. Do not use the words: like, bad, dislike, worst, hate, or horrible. ●● ●●	List 2 songs. For each describe the emotion or tone of voice. For example: "Happy Birthday to You" – Joyful and full of excitement. Choose one of the songs and describe how the words could be sung with a different voice and meaning. ●●● ●●	Draw two pictures of the same scene from a story or your own life. Use colors to represent very different moods. ●● ● ●●

*Set up activity: Students wrote their meaning of voice and shared in a class discussion.

Figure 7.2. Example: Tiered Version Two. Former excerpt from http://www.randomhouse.com/kids/junieb/letter/letter.html

Analysis and Reflection

The teacher designed the first Think Dot at the level equal to what she wanted all students to achieve. Next, she reviewed the tasks compared to student achievement data. Realizing that some students would struggle beyond a helpful point with the tasks, she constructed a second version of the Think Dot. The students were grouped by readiness level based on academic assessment data, and given the Think Dot that best meet their needs.

This Think Dot activity is tiered because of the two versions of the task that encourage students to work at an appropriate academic stretch. There are other characteristics exhibited in the tasks that attend to learning preferences, which will be studied in the respective chapter. Look closely at the different tasks and reflect on how the tasks are framed for thinking. The point for referencing this out now is to keep in mind that differentiation done well can have multiple layers. Some activities will be self-contained in a learner and teacher element, such as learning preferences and content, respectively. Other activities may contain a mix of multiple student and teacher elements.

Tiered activities may be focused on the same academic learning outcome, as is the case with this fractions example. Another version may address different academic learning outcomes when the learning gap is too wide to focus on the same content. This may occur when some students need to focus on concepts that are building blocks to the larger standard.

A simple tiered activity is taking an existing activity and making a new version. The new draft should meet the appropriate academic complexity for students who would find the current work easy and/or for the students who have gaps in their understanding that may prevent them from growing in the expected outcomes.

Example Three: Access to Understanding

In an elementary science class, students read articles about animal habitats and adaptations to the environment. The teacher provided a variety of reading materials on the topic. The materials were assigned to students based on their reading level. This approach gave students access to content at a written level that they could understand.

A high school English teacher had students reading *Animal Farm*. While some read silently to themselves, other students listened to audio recordings while following the printed text. After each reading, students would answer questions for comprehension and exploring the themes, which they later shared with their table partners. The teacher moved among the students to assist them along the process as needed.

Analysis and Reflection

A common mistake is that students with gaps in communication skills, such as reading, writing, speaking, and paying attention, are viewed as not ready for the critical thinking required for some tasks. While a deficit in any of these communication skills certainly needs to be addressed, that should not be a reason to deny them opportunities to tackle complex concepts. Think of any person who has low-reading skills. Ask them for their opinion on a topic that they know much about. It is highly likely that they can give an in-depth opinion and critique about that topic. How is that possible when they do not read well? They find other ways to get access to the content.

This applies to the science teacher providing reading materials at different levels, and the English teacher offering the audio recordings to classic literature. These actions do not directly address the gaps in reading skills. That requires approaches for a different focus. Guided reading, reading apprenticeship, running records, and DRA kits are just some of the approaches to specifically improve reading skills. These teachers are attending to standards for habitats, adaptations, and literary analysis. Given the supports to access the content, students realize the parts of the curriculum that they can accomplish. This newfound confidence could be used as motivation to address the important needs of basic communication skills.

TEACHING READINESS THROUGH PROCESS

Teachers plan for how students make sense of the content. The differentiation element of process is an important focus when planning checks on students' understanding throughout a lesson. Building understanding through how a learner makes sense of information can be addressed through different opportunities to reflect and apply what they have been exposed to. The key to readiness and process is that there are different opportunities and options that target a range for growth.

Example One: Portioning Understanding

For a science lesson, students read several sections of a chapter using a version of the reading protocol, Save the Last Word for Me.[5] They repeated the entire process twice, once over the first half and then second half of the reading. The students were placed in teams of three to four. They participated in the following steps:

1. The team decided how far they would read, usually one to two pages.
2. While reading, they marked passages using sticky notes:
   √: Checkmark for an important passage that they already knew.

!: Exclamation mark for an important passage that was new learning to them or sparked a new idea.

?: Question mark for an important passage that they wanted more information about or needed clarification.

3. After reading the agreed-upon length, one member would share a passage that they marked, without additional explanation.
4. Each of the other participants responds to the passage with their thoughts about it. There is no cross-talk or interruptions.
5. The person who shared the passage shares last about why he or she chose the passage, having heard everyone's ideas first. There is no cross-talk or interruptions.
6. With a new person sharing a passage, repeat Steps 3 to 5.
7. Once everyone has had a turn, the team picks a new amount of reading, repeating all steps.

After completing the reading protocol, teams reported out key ideas. The teacher recorded ideas on a shared Google Doc.[6] The teacher fills in any gaps for essential understandings.

Analysis and Reflection

A common concern with reading assignments is comprehension. A danger is that students will read for completion, with surface understanding. They may remember the beginning or end but not so much of the key ideas from the body of the text. Protocols like Save the Last Word for Me, Say Something, and Three-Levels of Text are means for learners to practice reflection. The reading assignment is portioned into two or three parts, so that students can pause after each section to interact with the key concepts, as well as process what they understand and what they need clarified. Peer support is immediate throughout the structured conversation.

As a readiness approach, students can be grouped with a mixture of reading skills or similar reading levels. In the first instance, heterogeneous groups include participants who can clarify comprehension for others where needed, or read aloud the text for easier access, while others follow along with the written text. It is important to note here that all group members are expected to tackle the academic tasks, even if the aforementioned comprehension supports are included.

In the second instance, students grouped by similar reading skills should have an assignment that is leveled to their respective reading level. Each group may have different articles that address the same topic but are written at the appropriate level for comprehension by the group. As with the first instance, the intent is to provide the same level of instruction about the concepts, regardless of the reading level of text.

The teacher moves among the groups to monitor students following the protocol. They may provide guidance or model a response where needed. Ensuring that no cross-talk or interruptions happen is a critical part of the experience. Such breaches in the protocol will cause the conversation to go off task, losing the depth of comprehension and insights.

Example Two: Access to Understanding

After providing several math examples for solving equations as an introduction, the teacher had classwork that students would start in class. The expectation was that unfinished work would be completed at home if needed. Before starting students on the classwork, he gave the students a quick check assessment. He put five equations on the board. The first task was a simple version of the instructional concepts, with an emphasis on foundational skills. The second and third tasks targeted the skills at the level desired for the learning outcome. The fourth task was a more complex version of the instruction. The final task was for a concept that would not be taught for several days. The students were charged with completing at least three of the tasks.

He allowed over half of the class to choose which tasks they would tackle. Based on academic assessment data, he assigned the start points for a few students. Task one was assigned to some, while others were required to complete only task four and five.

The tasks took seven to ten minutes to complete. The teacher collected the work and quickly placed them into two piles. The first pile was for students ready to start on the classwork. The second pile was for students who the teacher met with for additional review of the concepts so that they became better equipped to do the classwork. For the few students who successfully tackled the fifth question, he gave them a different class assignment to puzzle out the new concepts. Included were links to video resources[7] to support their inquiry.

Analysis and Reflection

The Quick Check assessment is identical to the Exit Card or Ticket out of the Door. The difference is when it's used. A common mistake made in lessons is that process moments are not included. Teachers go from teaching content to providing classwork or homework that students must complete (product). The problem with this situation is that there are learners who may have an incomplete to no understanding of the content taught in the lesson. They start the classwork or homework and eventually run into an insurmountable obstacle.

In the case of classwork, the student could ask for help, or wait quietly for the lesson to close, thus ending what they feel is an uncomfortable feeling.

For homework assignments, these students may spend hours of frustration working on tasks that they simply lack the skills to accomplish, or avoid doing the work. The result is that the next day, there are students who are now a day behind the others. Until they get support, their understanding gap will widen. Also, their confidence in doing the work will erode until they equate failure with doing such work, leading to a self-fulfilling prophecy.

When the teacher does some type of quick assessment after content delivery, he learns which students are ready to do the classwork or homework, and which students need additional instructional support. Allowing those who are ready to move forward with assignments, while working with just the ones who need additional support, honors all learners. Reteaching to the whole class, when some already understand the concepts, creates a strain for students who feel that their time is being wasted. It's also not efficient use of time by the teacher. It is far better to work with the smaller group so as to differentiate for their needs, while allowing the others to move forward. The teacher in this example was cognizant of these ideas when he used the quick check.

The teacher offered a range of five tasks but the students had to complete only three. A range allows students to choose where their comfort level exists—empowers their voice. When time is limited, it is a mistake to require all students to complete all of the tasks.

The message to those who struggle is that it is more important to complete all tasks incorrectly than to show what is understood from completing a reasonable number of tasks within the time allowed. One parent expressed frustration at this pervasive attitude at the school her children attended, which is more common than perhaps is realized. "Whether teachers realize it or not, completion is more important than understanding." Often unintended by the teachers, an outcome is that parents ask their children "Did you do your homework?" more often than "What did you learn today?"

Some students were required to complete the first task because the teacher wanted to check on their foundational knowledge. Prior assessments may have indicated some suspicions of needed instruction. The first task helps the teacher to confirm such suspicions.

Some advanced students were assigned, without choice, the last two tasks. This ensures that students who need a different challenge do not take the easy route of completing tasks that they already know. It's an opportunity to stretch students for growth that they need.

Why do they have only to do two tasks when others are required to complete three? The teacher calculated that completing the two tasks will take as much time as it takes everyone else to complete the three tasks of their choosing. Any student can try the fifth task. The intent of the quick check is determining who is ready to move forward with the classwork, and who needs additional support before they tackle the assignment, or is in need of a different more appropriate complex work.

TEACHING READINESS THROUGH PRODUCTS

Products provide opportunities for formative assessment on what students understand and do not know. When differentiating products, it's important to keep the learning outcome in mind. If the focus is on developing the building blocks toward the main standard expectation, then students might complete tiered assignments where some students may work on more fundamental skills, while others practice further along the continuum of the standard.

The expectation is that students working on more foundational skills are being guided toward eventually mastering the outcomes that everyone is expected to do. Other readiness experiences will provide various product options. Some will have included supports that help students bridge the non-assessed communication skills so as to work with the assessed content. Leveled readers, audio recordings, and graphic organizers are some examples.

Example One: Supports: Ranged Complexity

During a literacy unit, the teacher and students read aloud an adapted version of *Little Red Riding Hood*. They did several activities to build comprehension and explored different messages from the story, such as listening to parents, caution with strangers, and families. Students discussed and journaled throughout the unit of study.

Finally, the teacher presented a RAFTs activity. The purpose was for students to show their understanding of themes and skills by using details to support their ideas.

RAFTs stands for role, audience, format, and topic with a strong verb.[8] Students choose a RAFTs where they take the assigned role, and think how best to write to their audience. The format is the frame that the answer will take shape in, such as a chart, script, or narrative draft. The topic is the heart of the concept, which is the focus of the writing assignment. Include a strong verb in the topic so as to create an active call to action by the writer.

The teacher assigned pairs of RAFTs to students based on assessment data regarding their understanding of theme and writing construction of details. In the RAFTs activity, the pairs from basic complexity to advanced complexity respectively were the first two rows, the third and fourth rows, and the last two rows. Once assigned rows, the students chose which RAFTs they would complete.

In some cases, students did not like their option. The teacher negotiated with them on changes to role, audience, and/or format so that students liked their options, while ensuring that the learning outcomes were met. Students worked on their individual choices. On the following day, they are put into groups of three. Using a checklist for details, they reviewed each other's draft and gave feedback about what was present and what could be added. Students then revised their RAFTs.

Table 7.2.   RAFTs Tiered Activity

Role	Audience	Format	Topic
Red	Police	Deposition or plot chart	Tell what really happened.
Grandma	Red	1–2 minute conversation (script)	Save lives. Don't talk to strangers.
Wolf	Defense attorney	1–2 minute conversation (script)	Help me! I was framed!
Neighbor	PTO	Flyer	Strangers & Red: Beware! (A Cautionary Tale)
Red	Friends	Obituary	Confess: A lesson I did not learn . . .
Wolf	Oprah	Memoir letter	Save me! I'm misunderstood.

Simple to complex from the first option to the last.
Focus: Understand themes from *Little Red Riding Hood*.
Task: Choose one of the following. Answer the topic giving 2–3 reasons, with details for each.

Analysis and Reflection

The teacher could have offered two or three choices that all students choose from. This type of choice-based activity could attend to interest but not readiness. The RAFTs options are crafted at different levels of complexity. The first two rows ask the learner to report details in sequential order as they happen. The second set of RAFTs options requires writers to take a stand and determine which main ideas will support their case. The final set of RAFTs options requires writers to incorporate more varied types of details such as examples and illustrations. The explanations will tend to be longer because of the need for elaboration for answering the topics.

While each student worked with RAFTs that aligned with his or her skill development for details, the teacher offered some flexibility in revising the RAFTs based on a learner's interests. The negotiation process also addressed readiness by coaching and supporting students with revising the RAFTs in ways that helped better understand and accomplish the task.

Any product can be tiered. The first step is to design the activity that meets the learning outcome at the level that all students should attain. Then design versions of the same product that addresses concepts with supports, from review of foundational skills to expansion of more advanced skills. Each support depends on the needs of that group of students.

Example Two: Options with a Range of Supports

Students worked on multiplication from single to multi-digit calculations. The teacher showed a humorous movie clip of two zany characters, Ma and Pa Kettle,[9] solving 25 × 5 incorrectly. The teacher led students in "sleuth" talk to explain the errors in the logic of the Kettle's reasoning based on their three proofs. Having solved the mystery of 25 × 5, the students soon work on an assignment with five multiplication problems.

Depending on the needs, sometimes the teacher assigned sets of problems based on skill needs. Other times she gave the same problem set to all of the students, either to work on individually or in pairs. The teacher included links to videos of herself explaining the multi-step process for 2+ digit multiplication, such as 25 × 12, 182 × 56. There were also links to math videos by others as an alternative option.

Based on formative assessment, the teacher did a mini-lesson with students who have struggled with place value and following the two-step process. She taught them the Lattice Method to help these students make the necessary connections, before sending them to complete the work.

Analysis and Reflection

When learners produce products that show their understanding, supports may be needed as guides or references that students use as needed. The math lesson includes a variety of such supports. Videos, mini-lessons, and learning partners were combined to provide students with ways for thinking through the tasks. If stuck, they could make use of the supports available to them from the reference videos, their peers, and the teacher.

The key to peer and teacher support is that the answer is not given, but drawn from the learner. In an AP College math course, students tackled complex algorithms along with a partner. Several times students approached the teacher to get verification if their work was progressing correctly.

Showing patience, the teacher would ask concept-based questions for which when students answered they were able to self-determine if their work was correct. Several of these advanced students struggled to answer the questions. The teacher would respond with a different question that embedded some fundamental essential understanding. Eventually, the students found the answer themselves from the conversation. The teacher never took the easy route of saying, "Yes, that's correct." It took more time to have these conversations but the result was deeper understanding and greater student confidence.

In both experiences, 2+ digit multiplication and the AP course, the teachers tasked students with products that all students were expected to complete.

They used different layers of support depending on the needs of each student's to stretch themselves toward the learning outcome. Such supports can be used with absolutely any high-quality product option and serves the learning needs of all skill levels.

FINAL THOUGHTS

Differentiating through readiness is a common need for all learners and an ongoing challenge for teachers. At numerous workshops and coaching sessions, an often-stated concern for teaching through readiness is the time commitment. On paper, such implementation does take time. Educators should ask themselves, "If I use readiness as a factor in lesson planning, are there likely more students who will have a better chance of making gains in learning then if the effort is not made?" The opinion of this author is that the answer will be: Yes.

Consider that when students fall behind in the curriculum, teachers and schools struggle with how to close the achievement gap. Now, more time is needed for reteaching and remedial support. Add to this struggle that the students needing the support may begin to give up on themselves as having the capacity to do the work and on the teachers as having the skills to help them. In this scenario, teachers not only have to teach the curriculum but they also need to mediate the student's perception about the curriculum. Why not put that time in upfront and reduce the amount of reteaching that is needed, and avoid student apathy that is generated by the educator system.

Thoughtful planning and implementation of readiness through content, process, and product can pay dividends of increased student achievement and confidence. Keep in mind that the teacher frames the content, processes, and products experiences. How they include and accommodate students' readiness needs determine how learners choose to go with the program or resist. Student engagement and apathy regarding readiness is influenced by how the learning experiences send messages of realistic support and encouragement.

INVITATIONS TO REFLECTION

As a result of this chapter, use the lens for differentiation to consider the following questions for a self-guided exploration of your practice and those whom you support.

1. Review the suggested strategies shared in this chapter for use in content, process, or product. Also find more strategies at www.SoAllCanLearn.

org. How might you use one or two strategies to meet learner needs of all your students?

2. Why do assessments for learning play a key role in effective use of differentiation through readiness?
3. Explain the difference between readiness that is tiered and readiness based on supports? How might they be used together and/or separately?
4. Why are readiness activities that address process so little used despite its critical value?
5. How much influence does or should readiness have on activities that are based on interests and/or learning preferences?
6. What will be your next step for including, improving, or expanding differentiation through readiness in your work with students and colleagues?

Crossroad Planning Invitation

- Design or revise a learning activity that focuses on readiness. Use one of the elements: content, process, and/or product as your focus.
- Facilitate a group or staff dialogue about readiness. Generate a list of 20+ strategies or ways to differentiate existing strategies based on readiness.

Enrichment Option

While completing the aforementioned task, include one or more of the following, as referenced throughout the book:

- Student Voice
- Formative assessment cycle
- Three-dimensional instruction frame

NOTES

1. Dayna Laur is the author of the excellent book, *Authentic Learning Experiences: A Real-World Approach to Project-Based Learning.* Authentic learning experience supports student voices through differentiated instruction. She has a more recent publication along with coauthor Jill Ackers, *Developing Natural Curiosity through Project Based Learning: 5 Strategies for the PreK-3 Classroom.* Both books are published by Routledge.

2. Grant Wiggins and Jay McTighe. *Understanding By Design*, Expanded 2nd edition.

3. Tools like EdPuzzle and Zaption enable teachers and students to chunk videos with built-in pauses for reflection on content, answering questions, or lead discussion

on the content. When ready, the video is unpaused and continues showing content until the next stoppage. As of this publication, find more information at www.EdPuz zle.com and www.Zaption.com. For all resources pertaining to this book, go to www. SoAllCanLearn.org.

4. Internal thinkers is an approach for making sense of ideas and concepts. This is addressed in the chapter focusing on learning preferences.

5. Patricia Averette. Save the Last Word for Me protocol. National School Reform Faculty. http://www.nsrfharmony.org/system/files/protocols/save_last_word_0.pdf. A similar protocol is Say Something. Learn about this and other protocols at www. SoAllCanLearn.org.

6. Google Doc is a cloud-based word processor. It can be shared out to anyone who has access to the link to the page. There are other cloud-based tools that serve a similar purpose. OneNote and other tools can be found to explore on www.SoAllCan Learn.org.

7. Schools have access to many video resources from a variety of websites and textbook companies. Khan Academy is a common resource that students can find a variety of concepts explained with demonstrations.

8. There is much written about RAFTs. Here is one resource: John McCarthy. RAFTs—Engaging to Differentiating Writer's Voice. http://openingpaths.org/blog/ 2014/10/rafts-packed/.

9. There are several postings of this video on such sites as YouTube. Use the search keywords: Ma Pa Kettle Math. Or find a link version at www.SoAllCanLearn.org.

Chapter 8

Differentiation in Practice: Interests for *All*

I like that we got to learn from other students who talk at our level.
The best thing about Edcamp is that we got to learn in detail about other people's passions.
The best thing about edcamp is all the creativity that people have.
—Voices of fifth graders from Serene Hills Elementary School

The best learning experiences are ones that the learner is interested in exploring. They share a vested interest in pursuing the topic, investigating, researching, and crafting products. Difficult concepts are represented in ways that make sense to the learner's life experiences. There are practical representations and applications presented that students understand and value. Using the interests of learners as a lens for differentiation helps students see how abstract concepts appear in areas of their passions and life experiences. For example, explore how the laws of motion can be applied to a favorite sport, or apply argument skills to issues in the online gaming world, such as League of Legends. League of Legends and E-Sports.

On the surface, this idea may seem alien to educators in practice. Instruction is designed by the teacher based on the curriculum guide and standards. A reading of such documents makes apparent how abstract are the concepts and skills represented. Such documents seek to get to the heart of the concepts and skills that teachers must teach to students, which may be most helpful for the teacher's understanding of the curriculum that must be delivered. What is often lacking is a translation for how to make sense from the students' perspectives.

The best curriculum, the highest-quality design of instruction, as determined by educators has little guarantee of learner buy-in when students are not involved in the planning or their ideas are not gathered and incorporated. Consider this situation:

During a number of visits at different middle and high schools that experiment with different instructional approaches such as project-based learning, STEAM/STEM, and authentic learning experiences, students were asked about their learning experiences. Responses varied depending on the quality of implementation, yet there were certain common threads regardless of location. They said:

- "I like having the support of others (peers). I don't have to suffer alone. Someone is there for me."
- "Having experts from outside of school to talk to is cool. It makes the work more interesting."
- "I like helping the community. Sometimes we work on a community problem. We get to present our solutions to a community organization."
- "I wish the teacher would let me choose how I want to present my ideas."
- "I'd like to maybe come up with my own topic."

Students express value in learning experiences where their voice matters to the work. Given a say in what is learned and how that learning is expressed can raise student willingness to be actively involved.[1] When the students were asked, "What if you could spend time doing something that you're passionate about outside of school—like four-wheeling, fishing, gaming, video production, or sports—and get academic credit at the same time?" Students agreed that, yes, they would like that. Several students' eyes widen, and one would ask, "Is that possible?" or "Can we really do that?"

INTERESTS GUIDELINES

The answer is yes! The first step depends on the teachers' comfort zone with being uncomfortable. They must trust in the capacity of their students to step up to the challenge, which they often do when given the chance. It is fine for the teacher to know less about the tools and technology that the student proposes using. There is much that can be learned from the students as they progress along their journey.

To foster student voice into learning, consider the following for reflection and guidance:

1. Be clear on the learning outcomes. Communicate these concretely to the learners.
2. Create a draft of the post assessment for the outcomes
3. Draft the initial learning experience.
   Include the learners in this shaping (preferred), otherwise go to Step 4.
4. Review student interest data from the learning profile cards and/or other data for adaptations or personalization.

5. Revise the learning experience and post assessment.
   Include the learners in this shaping (preferred), otherwise, offer an additional option where students can propose alternative ideas for the work products and assessment.
6. Implement and reflect. Follow the formative assessment cycle (FAC).

Learning experiences informed by student interests can lead to greater involvement and investment. The idea seems like good common sense, so what prevents its extended use? Time and control are commonly raised concerns.

Table 8.1. Interests-Based Examples

Learners are motivated or self-determine action by how learning experiences are structured. They are likely to participate when one or more of these areas are met: readiness, interests, and/or learning preferences.	**Interests** Develop learning experiences based on the learners' background and feedback: • Choice • Learning profile • Hobbies and pursuits
Content How is access to information made for learners? How are learners able to access and understand the concepts and skills?	• Jigsaw materials • Learning contracts • "Say Something" or "Last Word" for readings • Present through multimedia • Centers: Choice of what content to study or study options within a center • Connect to student lives/world beyond classroom (context)
Process How can learners digest content and make into their own?	• Choose work based on learning profile such as Sternberg MI or brain-based • Centers: Students choose options for how they will do the task • Group by like-interests • Think Dots • Project/problem-based learning • Independent study/projects • Writer's workshop • Web quest
Product How would learners distill what they learned by application, demonstration, or performance?	• Sternberg MI activity • RAFTS: Work is chosen, and/or is based on interest • Built-in options with connection to interests • Project/problem-based learning • RAFTS • Rubric-based activities • Design something

But both are rooted in trusting students to do what is asked of them, which is more likely to happen if they are included in the work that affects them.

The illusion is that curriculum coverage assumes that learning has taken place for all students. It does not. Curriculum delivery is what teachers can control and shows what has been accomplished—by the teacher. When learner growth is the focus, students must be included in at least some of the decisions about their learning experiences. As referenced with adult learners, when students are given voice in their work, they are more likely to have investment in the experience. Start with using a tool like the learning profile cards, discussed in a previous chapter. Gather data about students from their perspective. What follows are examples that range in student voice, supported by differentiation through interests.

TEACHING INTERESTS THROUGH CONTENT

Choices and embedding interest topics are some ways to differentiate content around interests. Get students to want to do the heavy lifting of research and unpacking understanding by framing the learning experiences that include areas where they can insert their own ideas, contribute to the understanding of others, and showcase their insights. Sometimes including a social component can be important as students make sense of content, and exchange ideas.

Example One: Lyrics as Poetry Project

High school ninth graders studied literary elements through music lyrics. Students chose a music artist or group to explore. They listened to many songs, narrowing down their choice to three songs. They studied the lyrics for themes, symbolism, and word choice. Wrote journals and an essay about what they learned about their chosen musicians. Students engaged in lively discussions and remained entirely focused on the literary tasks set before them.

One young lady, in her final journal, reflected on being troubled about her chosen music group. Prior to the unit, she often played the music. During the unit, based on her analysis of the lyrics and themes, she felt confronted by the group's disrespect of women. Much of the music treated women as sex objects, whose primary role was to please men. The student found herself reconsidering if she would continue to listen to the band's music.

Analysis and Reflection

The music unit exemplifies the potential value of differentiation based on interests by giving students the reigns for what they study. A traditional approach would have the teacher leading the unit by selecting the artist and songs. Students would use the songs, selected by the teacher, to study the literary elements, for which they would feel less connection. For anyone who disagrees, consider that in most literature classes, the teacher chooses the novel, play, or poems. That is common practice. Yet, when students choose, they are likely to be more attentive. Literature Circles is one example, which will be explored in the section "Teaching Interests through Processes."

From a teacher's perspective, the success or failure of this music experience is the clarity of the learning outcomes and how students will address them through the instructional experiences. In this case, students chose the music artist or group and the songs. The related tasks strongly connected with the research skills and literary elements that made purposeful the learning experiences.

The student's reflection about her conflicted feelings of the music group she'd avidly followed in the past might not have occurred without her active participation. Had she done the same work about a musician of the teacher's choosing, she may still have done quality work, but the lack of relevance may likely not have had the same self-reflection. How many other music groups would she and others examine more closely? Consider how the skills firmly taught through this experience could be used as a platform for later more complex study.

Example Two: "Edcamp: Where Voice and Choice Matters"

At Lake Travis ISD, Cathy Hill recounts the work of a fifth grade team lead by Kathy Austrian and Amanda Reedy. The two-week experiences at Serene Hills Elementary culminated in a student-led Edcamp. Involving students in crafting the experience, provided students ways to differentiate for themselves. Here are Cathy's words:

Setting the stage for the students was a priority. Day 1, students arrived to butcher-papered hallways proclaiming, "What do you want to learn? Bring your passion! Bring your voice!" Students brainstormed topics they would like to learn about, writing on sticky notes and posting on the butcher paper. The hallway on Day 2 boasted the caption, "What will you teach? How will you inspire? Share your passion!" Students learned about different personality types and identifying strengths. This again led to discussions about passions, why people have different ones, and how to pursue them.

The remaining days leading to EdCamp included a variety of learning experiences. Students wrote proposals that included learning outcomes, identified materials needed (technology, props, etc.), and outlined presentations with time limits for each section. They learned about asking questions that prompt higher-order thinking and about facilitating discussion. They also practiced some classroom management skills to regain the attention of their audience, if needed. In the two days prior to EdCamp, students had the opportunity to practice their presentations, receiving feedback from the teacher and students in their classroom.

The eventful day arrived. A banner proclaiming, "Edcamp—Where Voice and Choice Matter" greeted the excited students. Young presenters shared passions, such as creating Harry Potter Potions, Mysteries of the Deep, Channeling Your Inner YouTube, Advanced Bicycles, Bonjour-Learn about France, Tricky to Please-Architecture and Design, Flippin' Fun Gymnastics, Flowering Photography, Personal Finance and Business, Oncology, The Cupcake Fanatic, 3-D Printing, and Acting with a Twist.

Quiet students came alive when talking about their passions. Inclusion students shared their passions and received high praise from their peers. Students learned about themselves and others, about interests and strengths that were previously unrecognized. Teachers were simultaneously exhausted and exhilarated. Students were given voice and choice—and it was incredible.

Analysis and Reflection

In the professional world of Education, EdCamps are a way for educators to gather around shared passions and common concerns. They signed-up for the topics that interested them, and participate in the learning. It is differentiation in action. The fifth grade teachers and Cathy Hill at Serene Hills Elementary saw that if such experiences were good for teachers, why not offer the same opportunities to their learners?

Students practiced research skills and organizing ideas for their presentations around topics that they care about. The act of choosing the topics for preparation at the EdCamp places accountability on the students. Consider the time students chose to spend on developing their communication skills because the topic was something they cared about.

Such an event requires logistical planning. How the teachers organized the work and pulled off the event with the help of 180 students is documented in an article by Cathy Hill, found in the Appendix. The EdCamp concept need not be as ambitious to get started. Running such an experience with one classroom can be quite successful if the planning is placed on one teacher. With more teachers involved in the process for their students, the experience can grow.

TEACHING INTERESTS THROUGH PROCESSES

When students get to choose what they talk about and/or how that conversation will take place, there can be a rich exchange of ideas and perspectives.

Other times, embedding into an activity a nonverbal form of communication that may be unfamiliar to students can create interest in experiencing something new or different. The key is that the experience is one that helps students reflect and explore their understanding for accuracies, enlightenments, and growth needs.

Example One: Literature Circle Conversations

Seventh grade students participated in a Literature Circle (Harvey Daniels).[2] They sat in groups of four or five. Each group had chosen a novel from a list of options available at the school. Based on their selection, the teacher differentiated by placing them into like-interest teams. Because ten students chose the same book, the teacher formed two teams.

One group asked if they could read a novel that was not on the list. At first, the teacher said no because there were no copies of the book in the school. The students had researched the book and found it for less than $4 as a Kindle e-book. They offered to buy it themselves. The teacher hesitated, torn between the students' apparent interest in the book and the potentially delicate issue of letting students pay for instructional materials. Seeming to sense her indecision, the students showed that they'd already bought the book. The teacher approved their book choice. A surprising benefit was that the students added notes and highlighted text on their e-books, which made for easy reference. The teacher supporting the students' lead on book selection helped to foster student voice in the classroom.

Within each group, students chose roles for preparation of the Literature Circle conversations:

- Passage Master

    This person collected three or more passages from the reading that were important to the storyline, themes, and/or author's craft.
- Illustrator

    This artist created a thoughtful image that depicted an important moment in the reading. The image could be hand crafted or digital.
- Quote Master

    This researcher collected three or more quotes from the reading that highlighted something about the character, story situation, or author's craft.
- Connections Manager

    This individual found relevance from at least two parts of the reading to incidents or events happening in the community or the news.
- Circle Facilitator

    The facilitator kept everyone on task with the discussion, and encouraged the others to share some of their findings to help keep the conversation alive.

During the course of the meeting experiences, students had to take on at least three of the roles.

Analysis and Reflection

Literature Circles have two strong connections with interests. When students choose the book or article there is greater buy-in. In the aforementioned example, teachers usually provide the choices, which can work well if there are enough options that students can choose from. In some instances, students might prefer or need options not on the list. Typically, this might be challenging due to funding. Where possible consider funding sources such as the parent organization that supports the school. Ask the building principal for assistance, as sometimes they have discretionary funds for small requests. At some schools, the parent community may be willing to offer support.

The second connection to interest are the roles. Allow students to decide which role they will take on for an activity. Requiring students to do three of the five roles during the course of the school year was reasonable as they could avoid some roles that did not interest them. Let the team decide the distribution of roles with the caveat that they must support each other, and not leave anyone feeling very uncomfortable with their role. The roles have specific preparation needs that help each student build understanding of the reading, and to help each other during the conversation to further process their understanding.

Some teachers who use literature circles might use roles minimally. The value of having some form of roles from a differentiation lens is the structure it provides, which can be of value to learners. If the emphasis is placed on students choosing the roles it can support their voice. An important value to the roles is that the students can practice the college and career readiness skills such as agency through collaboration, communication, critical thinking, and problem solving.

Example Two: Affinity Mapping Protocol

In a high school government course, the teacher led several lessons on the branches of government, using primary source documents and contemporary articles about critiques of actions by each of the branches. In preparation for the students' research to form their own critical analysis, the teacher sets up an affinity mapping protocol[3] as a means for students to explore their understanding and that of their peers. In the room are eight chart papers taped to walls. There are four prompts, one on each chart paper. The prompts are duplicated on a second set of chart paper, resulting in eight in total. The two sets of chart paper are to manage the approximate 35 students involved.

The topics written are:

1. Explain the roles and critique of the judiciary.
2. Explain the roles and critique of the legislature.
3. Explain the roles and critique of the executive.
4. Explain the values and challenges of checks and balances.

Students chose the chart topic that they were most interested in. Each chart could only have a maximum of four students. Students who could not join a full team, chose a different chart as their home base. Each student held nine sticky notes and a pen.

Phase One: At the teacher's signal, the teams rotated to the next chart paper. They wrote two to three responses to the prompt. They worked in silence. At the teacher's signal, students posted their notes and moved to the next chart paper. The process repeated for all three prompts, and then the students returned to their home base.

Phase Two: At the teacher's signal, students reviewed the sticky notes and moved them around the chart paper into clusters, based on common connections. They worked together in silence. Any sticky note moved by one person could be moved by another.

Phase Three: At the teacher's signal, the students decide on labels to represent the clusters. They are allowed and encouraged to talk. Sticky notes can be moved between clusters or form new clusters for the purpose of creating labels.

Phase Four: Each team reports to the class about their decisions for the clusters and the related meaning. What followed was dialogue where students reflected on the ideas expressed for any of the topics and their implications.

After the discussion, students wrote a reflection journal based on open-ended prompts by the teacher. While the teacher reviewed the reflections, the students began planning their research topic.

Analysis and Reflection

The affinity mapping protocol includes choice as students determine their home base. The other charts are used to generate content during each rotation. The prompts should be open so that students have latitude on the possible ideas to express. Silent and verbal communication incorporates learning preferences where students get to experience both, with at least one approach fitting into their comfort zone. Experiencing both enables all students to have at least one connection with which they are familiar. The silent component ensures that all voices are "heard" through the silent dialogue of contributing ideas during the rotations and organizing sticky notes into clusters.

The teacher prepped for success by building a knowledge base through various lessons. The affinity mapping helped to inform what students understood and clarify through their peers the areas they may have had struggles. The process offers opportunities for epiphanies, inspired by the generated responses and clustering. Students are better prepared to choose their topic and generate research questions after having such an experience to reflect and process their ideas and those of their peers.

TEACHING INTERESTS THROUGH PRODUCTS

Products are a good place to start exploring differentiating through interests. These are the concrete creations that students make that tie to formative assessments. Start with giving choices. Expand by embedding their interests in the choices. Eventually, develop frameworks for facilitating collaborative dialogue where students propose their own product ideas that can reflect the learning outcomes.

Example One: L12 Capstone Project-Based Learning

At the Center for Innovation[4] at Lapper Community Schools in Michigan, the Senior Capstone is a one-year project-based learning environment. Through a variety of experiences, the seniors explore many topics with the ultimate goal of them designing and implementing their own capstone learning experience.

In the spring, seniors worked on the philanthropy project.[5] Here is what the document that launched the learning experience stated:

> You and your team mates work for Facebook. Mark Zuckerberg needs to donate his money to a nonprofit, and he has assembled you all to figure out where to donate his millions. You and your team are to create a professional boardroom presentation that defines your chosen social issue and, through persuasive efforts, explains why that issue should be the recipient of his fortunes.[6]

Students formed teams based on a shared interest for a philanthropy idea. Team sizes varied from one to five. Topics ranged widely, such as domestic violence or the water crisis in Flint, Michigan. The task was to either raise actual funds to donate to their cause, purchase product of equal value, or contribute service hours.

One team procured donations of cases of water bottles to assist with the Flint water crisis. Another team visited local rural homes that had wells. They offered to test the water quality of the wells for free. If the water was in the parameters for drinking, the students asked the owners for permission to fill the water jugs they brought with them for the intent of delivering to water stations in Flint.

Students produced a research paper about their cause. They created a promotional presentation through digital media such as a podcast or public service announcement (PSA). Many of the students talked about their cause with a depth of knowledge and understanding. They expressed pride in what they were able to accomplish.

Analysis and Reflection

Senior Capstone programs are effective when students are empowered to develop their focus. In this case, the seniors got to choose their cause. The teachers included many checkpoints that students had to accomplish to show progress. Where students fell short, the teachers were able to use the checkpoints to identify the appropriate support.

> The philanthropy project has been the favorite project of both years we've implemented it. The biggest appeal, I think, is that students get to choose who they help, and that is a powerful motivator. We try to build student choice in all parts of our projects because, really, that is what gets students to invest themselves into their learning." Melissa Campbell, L12 Capstone Teacher

The products were tightly aligned to English content standards and for Global Success Skills.[7] Students could also negotiate the product options, so long as the results met the learning outcomes. When considering doing a similar experience in any classroom, it is possible to start with a small assignment. Be clear about the skills and concepts that must be applied. Provide a clear checklist of the progression of work that helps the teacher and students to check-in on the progress. Set loose the students. With an experience that is one to two lessons, the teacher can coach students on how to take their interests to great heights. Students are motivated when they can choose what they want to do and get credit for it.

Example Two: Third Law of Motion— Student-Directed Exploration

Kristen Kohli, a science teacher at Estrella Foothills High School, had students study the third law of motion: For every action there is an equal and opposite reaction. Having spent time studying the law through teacher instruction, students worked in teams to generate five field-tested demonstrations of Newton's third law. Each team captured these experiments via video (phones and computers). The videos were put into PowerPoint. The files were uploaded to Edmodo.com[8] in an assignment drop box. The students shared their work for review the following day.

When asked about the value of learning experience, Kristen Kohli explained:

> What I really enjoyed most about doing this lesson with the students was watching their enthusiasm and creativity blossom. They seemed to relish the competition—trying to come up with the most original ideas for demonstrating the third law, and then managing to capture that idea on video. For them it seemed less about the grade and more about impressing each other with a great shot and me with something no one else had thought of. Some of the clips were funny, some were highly over-engineered, but all of the students walked away with a clear understanding of how the law worked and how to recognize it when they saw it. I think they appreciated being given ownership over what they were going to do and having the chance to do something novel.

Analysis and Reflection

The students chose the different types of experiments that they would conduct. The teacher provided a variety of tools, such as rubber bands, sports scooters (a 16" board on four wheels), plastic spoons, and balloons. Students had an open-ended approach to the experiment. The students discussed and debated different ideas within their teams. The dialogue was mostly the language of science.

The teacher could have given a test, assigned a paper, or given her own set of experiments. The outcome would not have fully engaged all the students. Every team attempted different experiments. When some failed, they would try a modification or explore a different idea. Some students did watch what others did for ideas, but ultimately they had to replicate those experiments successfully. Their video of themselves was their evidence of success.

Example Three: Poetry Pallooza

Beth Rayl champions student voice throughout her career as a teacher and administrator. During her ongoing support of teachers, she designed a learning experience that was packed with interest-based differentiation for support of students.

Name: Beth Rayl
  Grade Level or Admin Position—Teacher Consultant
  Subject: Health, PE, History, Reading, Administration

Complete the following:

Insert two social media tools into a lesson series for students (children or adults). Include a learning support experience using resources and/ or referenced information from two social media tools. For example, include video from TeacherTube, an article from a blogger, or a podcast.

1. Lesson Series Topic: Poetry Palooza (Analyzing and Interpreting a Poem)
2. Key Learning Outcome focus: Students will create a podcast, iMovie, blog, or other project to analyze and interpret a poem.

    My original design for this lesson prior to adding the social media tools can be found at: https://www.commonsense.org/education/lesson-plans/poetry-palooza
3. Global Competency Focus: Collaboration:

    Students will collaborate as a member of a team to develop, create, and share their analysis and interpretation via a social media tool. Students will also collaborate with other students from a "sister school" to share and discuss their interpretations of the chosen poems.
4. Social Media Tool 1: Blogger (www.blogger.com)

    Students will set up a blog to collaborate on and discuss their analysis and interpretation—first within their team and then with students from the sister school in another state or country.
5. Social Media Tool 2: Podcast

    Once students have collaborated upon their poetry analysis both internally (classroom) and externally (another school), they will create a podcast to share their reflections on the chosen poetry. This podcast will include an interview with a poet. Once completed, the podcast will be shared on the class website.

Reflection: How will the chosen Social Media tools support student learning?

The use of a blog for collaboration will encourage students to engage in ongoing dialogue with a purpose, in this case to analyze and interpret poetry. Students will be encouraged to develop and share their "voice" by communicating with both classroom colleagues and others beyond the classroom walls. Having the students create a podcast allows them to develop speaking and listening skills. Students will spend time in advance discovering what makes a "good" podcast. Through blogging and podcasting in this project, students will be enhancing their oral and written communication skills.

Beth Rayl rationale for this type of interests-based learning experience is best explained in her own words:

> It's important for us, as educators, to give students a voice and choice in their learning. This enables students to truly show what they know. Throughout my career, when I allowed students to demonstrate learning in authentic ways they always amazed me with their depth of thinking about and understanding of content.

Analysis and Reflection

Students reviewed elements of poetry by reading and discussing works from different authors. They used social media tools to expand access to readings and listening to recordings. In schools where resources are limited, digital access opens up opportunities to align student interests, in this case, to poetry that they may relate to.

Digital tools were also important for students to have access to a wider audience and to practice collaboration skills among their peers and professionals in the field. The core content expectations remain the same. Through social media tools, students have more opportunities for personalized learning. The learning outcomes should not be compromised, as the tools used to demonstrate learning is reviewed prior to use. Create a win-win experience (Stephen Covey).[9]

FINAL THOUGHTS

There are many ways to incorporate choice as indicated in the aforementioned examples. Choice and open-ended options work well where the teacher identifies the learning outcomes and a list of checkpoints. Such structures help keep learners organized and focused on the outcomes.

Other tools like Think Dots, RAFTs, and Learning Menus can also be used to give students options for how they do work. Using such tools as Learning Profile cards, discussed in an earlier chapter, is the next level of developing interest-based learning experiences. Such an assessment about student interests informs the teacher's decision for how options are shaped.

Of course, one of the best forms of information gathering is a direct conversation with the student. Negotiating with them on how they want to learn content, process understanding, and craft products can raise student buy-in and accountability because they help make the decisions. Not every student will need or want such a conversation. As teachers get to know their students, they will be able to determine the level of choices and voice each learner needs.

INVITATIONS TO REFLECTION

As a result of this chapter, use the lens for differentiation to consider the following questions for a self-guided exploration of your practice and those whom you support.

1. Review the suggested strategies shared in this chapter for use in content, process, or product. Also find more strategies at www.SoAllCanLearn. org. How might you use one or two strategies to meet learner needs of all your students?
2. Why do assessments play a key role in effective use of differentiation through interests?
3. Why are process interests approaches so little used despite its critical value?
4. How much influence does or should Interests have on activities that are based on readiness and/or learning preferences?
5. What will be your next step for including, improving, or expanding differentiation through interests in your work with students and colleagues?

Crossroad Planning Invitation

• Design or revise a learning activity that focuses on interests. Use one of the elements: content, process, and/or product as your focus.
• Facilitate a group or staff dialogue about interests. Generate a list of 20+ strategies or ways to differentiate existing strategies based on interests.

Enrichment Option

While completing the aforementioned task, include one or more of the following, as referenced throughout the book:

• Student Voice
• Formative assessment cycle
• Three-dimensional instruction frame

NOTES

1. As referenced in Chapter 6 regarding adult learners could be applied to students in the pre-k to 12 world in regards to student voice.

Learning Forward on Standards for Professional Learning. https://learning forward.org/standards/learning-designs. The Pew Research Center did a survey of adults. *Lifelong Learning and Technology* by John Horrigan (March 22, 2016). The

responses were interesting in that personalized voice was prevalent. http://www.
pewinternet.org/2016/03/22/lifelong-learning-and-technology/.

2. Harvey Daniels is an important influencer for understanding and using literature
circles. He wrote, *Literature Circles: Voice and Choice in Book Clubs and Reading
Groups*, 2nd edition. Stenhouse Publishers. 2002.

3. Affinity Mapping is available at the National School Reform Faculty site: www.
nsrfharmony.org/system/files/protocols/affinity_mapping_0.pdf.

4. The Center for Innovation (http://cfi-west.lapeerschools.org/) contains many
programs for middle schoolers and high schoolers. The L12 Capstone is a program for
seniors, which is different from traditional schools. The culture is more like a college
campus with classrooms and open working spaces where students work individually
and in teams. http://lapeerseniorcapstone.weebly.com/.

5. The Philanthropy project can be found at http://lapeerseniorcapstone.weebly.
com/philanthropy.html.

6. This statement was the launch of the philanthropy project. http://lapeersenior
capstone.weebly.com/philanthropy.html.

7. The standards can be found at this link: http://lapeerseniorcapstone.weebly.com/
uploads/3/8/4/0/38409435/philanthropy_project_board1.pdf or on www.SoAllCan
Learn.org.

8. Edmodo is one of many online classroom structures. Some other options might
include Schoology.com, Google Classroom, and Coursesites.com.

9. Stephen Covey. *The 7 Habits of Highly Effective People: Powerful Lessons in
Personal Change.* Simon & Schuster. 2013. Excerpt from *Habit 4: Think Win-Win.*
https://www.stephencovey.com/7habits/7habits-habit4.php

Chapter 9

Differentiation in Practice: Learning Preferences for *All*

As teachers, it is our responsibility to help our students access the content in whatever modality is most effective for their enduring understanding of the material.

— Jennifer Allan, elementary/middle school teacher

Learning preferences are an important part of the instructional design process. Its value is in seeing and understanding learners from multifaceted points of view. The danger is the improper use of learning preferences by placing leaners into single categories for how they learn, as research does not support such practices (John Hattie).[1] See Chapter 5 for how concerns are addressed. People learn using a variety of approaches and perspectives that work for them. An individual may prefer visual elements in learning, and may also navigate instruction delivered through auditory means, and with introspection as part of the experience. Learners should not be limited to one avenue, but experience a variety, such as through three-dimensional instruction.

Collecting data on student learning preferences might at this point be mostly anecdotal. It may be based on observations by educators, parent feedback, and surveys and reflective perspectives by the learner. This data provide an image of what differentiation planning might occur.

There are many approaches to choose from, each having its fan base and argument for why it works well for learners. Some approaches include:

- Robert Sternberg's triarchic theory of intelligence
- Bernice McCarthy's 4-MAT
- Howard Gardner's theory of multiple intelligence

Other factors that could be placed into this arena are such works on brain-based learning, growth and fixed mind-sets, and internal and external

147

thinking approaches. Asking teachers to gather all of this data is destined for failure without an effective way to access the data for use.

LEARNING PREFERENCES GUIDELINES

Here are guidelines when planning for learning preferences:

1. Be clear on the learning outcomes. Communicate these concretely to the learners.
2. Create a draft of the post assessment for the outcomes
   If appropriate for the assessment, include at least two learning preferences as part of the whole experience, or use the learning preferences to create different versions. If there is more than one version, let the student choose the assessment they take.
3. Draft the initial learning experience.
   Include two or more learning preferences in this drafting (best option), otherwise go to Step 4.
4. Review student data from the learning profile cards and/or other data for adaptations or personalization.
5. Revise the learning experience and post assessment.
   Include the learners in this shaping (preferred), otherwise, offer an additional option where students can propose alternative ideas for the work products and assessment.
6. Implement and reflect. Follow the formative assessment cycle (FAC).

Using learning preferences can be challenging without an organization structure to collect and update. Learning profile cards is a strategy that supports teacher reflection on practice as they align the best instructional match for each student.

LEARNING PROFILE CARDS

Learning profile cards is a great strategy for collecting perceptual data about students' strengths in subjects and approaches to learning. Students self-evaluate so that their perspective is recorded about themselves as learners. Once completed, teachers can add annotated information about the students that further informs them on team formations that can lead to success with learning standards.

- Target Grades: All
- Activity Time: 15–20 minutes
- Materials: index cards and a pen or pencil (one per student)

Learning profile cards have been adopted by teachers of all grade levels. From personal experience and that of secondary teachers with over 100 students, the cards become essential. Considering how more challenging it is to get to know about all students on the roster, using this strategy is a way to get a jump-start on building that relationship. In less than 20 minutes of a class period, the teacher knows more about each of his students, then if he'd not done this activity.

Activity Steps

Step One

After passing out the index cards to each student, have them write on the back of the card their contact information. At a minimum, this would include their name and personal phone number.

The purpose of this information is for when student teams need to contact an absent member about work that needs to be submitted. Since it appears that students use e-mail far less, having other means of contact is important within social media.

Step Two

On the front of the card, the top corners and the bottom right corner are for tracking learning styles and personality inventories. Teachers choose any

---

Learning Profile Cards (Back)

Name:
Phone number:
Email:
Social media:

Figure 9.1.   Learning Profile Card (Back)

Learning Profile Cards (Front)

Learning Styles Preferences 1	**Thinking Styles**
i.e., R. Sternberg's Triarchaic Theory	:Internal
Analytical:	:External
Practical:	
Creative: List 3–4 interests,	
hobbies, other	
	:This course
Learning Styles Preferences 2	:Reading
i.e., H. Gardner's MI elements	:Writing
Kinesthetic:	:Math
Auditory:	:Science
Visual:	:Multimedia

Rate self on each section from 4 (high preference) to 1 (low preference)

Figure 9.2.   Learning Profile Card (Front)

style/inventory that they feel confident using for meeting their students' needs. For each learning styles/inventory categories used, the teacher should describe them in terms that relate to the students. For example, "If you see yourself as a visual learner, then when I ask for directions to the nearest sandwich store, you would give directions as you see yourself walking or driving there." Another option is to use an established inventory test to gather this data from students. Taking a test can take more time, which some teachers may be able to fit in the schedule.

Students use the four-point scale to self-assess for each category. It's important to track at least two. This helps to avoid typecasting students into one learning container. Such as, Dagan is a visual learner. That probably depends on the situation. More important, how would Dagan rate himself?

Step Three

In the center, students list three to four interests that they have outside of school. This could range from recording themselves as they play video games to talking or texting with friends. This information helps to relate the context of subject matter to things that matter to students. Also, when designing projects and lessons, teachers may create a learning experience around the interests of one to two students in the class. These are the students in danger of falling further behind, until they eventually lose faith in the education system and likely stop trying.

Step Four

In the bottom, right corner, students list the subjects and skills. For each, rate them from a 4, I'm great at this skill/subject and I love it, to a 1, I'm not very good at this skill/subject and I do not like it. Some teachers use a wider range such as an 8-point or 10-point scale. That's fine so long as the range is an even number. Otherwise, students tend to choose the middle number such as three out of five, or five out of nine.

It's also important to note that the score is far less important than the fact that the students rated themselves in the top half or bottom half. This speaks volumes about their perception of themselves, which we'll see repeated with the other categories to follow. When students rate themselves low in the teacher's course content area, it indicated the need to mediate the student's self-perception of their skills if they are going to build confidence with making an effort.

Step Five

Once the students complete the cards, the teacher collects them to use for making teams and differentiating lessons and projects. Because the students

Table 9.1. Learning Preferences-Based Examples

Learners are motivated or self-determine action by how learning experiences are structured. They are likely to participate when one or more of these areas are met: readiness, interests, and/or learning preferences.	**Learning Preferences** How a student approaches concepts from his or her strengths Lens for making sense and communicating through: • Multiple intelligence • Brain-based
Content How is access to information made for learners? How are learners able to access and understand the concepts and skills?	• Give material in perspective of multiple intelligences • Notes with highlighted important details • Graphic organizer: Data displayed through multiple intelligences • Present through multimedia • Centers: Provide content in different mediums

(Continued)

Table 9.1.   (Continued)

Process How can learners digest content and make into their own?	• Learning styles are incorporated in experiences, such as Sternberg MI or brain-based • Centers: Tasks are completed using different learning styles. Work is assigned or self-selected • RAFTS: Format options are based on multiple-intelligence • Group by same learning preference or include each thinking style • Think dots • Project/problem-based learning • Writer's workshop • Web quest
Product How would learners distill what they learned by application, demonstration, or performance?	• Sternberg MI activity • Think-tac-toe • Project/problem-based learning • Presentation formats • RAFTS • Contracts • Design something • Performance task

completed them, teachers should add or update information on the cards based on ongoing observations.

For early elementary students, teachers might bring in parents or student buddies from an upper grade level, who acts as the younger students' secretaries and transcribe their answers. This saves time.

TEACHING LEARNING PREFERENCES THROUGH CONTENT

When delivering content to diverse learners, an important step is to present content through multiple ways. John Hattie distinguishes expert teachers from experienced teachers, where the qualities of expert teachers demonstrate skills such as flexibility, improvisation, and reflective of practice.[2] The temptation of other teachers is to match delivery with what is perceived as economical of time. This decision places learners as a secondary consideration.

A helpful approach is to evaluate one's own comfort zone for instructional communication, and add other ways that might not be as comfortable for the teacher, but may be for learners. Consider ways that help learners make sense of content, even when it may disrupt the timelines established by others who envision a world where all students simply learn at the same pace. In the short term, more time may be used, but in the long term, the time is made up as fewer students struggle over the same content.

Example One: Three-Dimensional View of Content

Becky Gorinac, director of Early Childhood Education, supports her preschool teachers with lesson support. She designed a lesson for the study of birds.[3]

- Students participated in a KWL activity about birds.
- Performed guided research to learn more about birds.
- From a list of four videos, students watched several for additional research gathering.
- As a large group, the students wrote informative posts on the class Facebook page, which the teacher would transcribe.

Becky Gorinac stated, "Because children in preschool are very young, their use of social media will be supported by the classroom teachers. Children will brainstorm their questions and then with adult support, can research information, preview videos from YouTube, and then verbally share what they want posted on the Facebook page."

Analysis and Reflection

During the study of birds, the students studied the content through a variety of approaches:

- Reflection and dialogue through the KWL activity
- Guided research
- Visuals through the YouTube videos
- Dialogue and crafting posts for Facebook

The whole class explored the content through all of these activities. The differentiation is in the variety of mediums used to teach the concept. By providing several different experiences, all students are more likely to find some connection that helps them build understanding. The traditional approach of providing content in one way may likely leave groups of students feeling disconnected without support. Differentiation through learning preferences does not always have to be customized or personalized, so long as there are experiences that each learner connects with. A mix of approaches is a good thing.

Often, differentiation through learning preferences is easily connected to including interests. Including two or all three of the elements for differentiation makes a stronger learning experience. This preschool example demonstrates that through the students making their own research decisions about the birds being studied. Becky Gorinac explains:

> Young children enter preschool with a wide-range of background knowledge and experiences, making differentiation a way of life for a preschool educator. When children's interests are used as the foundation of embedded academic and social-emotional learning, preschoolers thrive. Enter any high-quality preschool program and you would never see worksheets being used. Instead, you will see groups of children engaged in varied literacy activities, such as pretending to be archaeologists digging letters out of the sand table, children writing menus for the restaurant they created in the house area, or sitting with the teacher in the library engrossed in a favorite book.

Preschoolers have a wide range of skill levels when they enter school. Becky Gorinac's reason in support of them is of equal value for quality learning for all the grade levels that follow. Authentic learning around areas of interest, while incorporating learning preferences helps develop experiences so all can learn.

Example Two: Window Activity

A teacher wanted students to become interested in studying the American Civil War as background for reading "The Red Badge of Courage" by Stephen Crane. After students read and discussed a short reading, using the say something protocol, the teacher led them through the Window Activity (Sally Jessup).[4]

The teacher showed on screen the first image, and said, "You are standing in a dark and empty room. There is only a window with the shade down. In a moment, I will raise the shade and you will see a picture of a scene. Describe what you see using the Fastwrite strategy."

The next slide showed the window frame with the shade raised. The picture was a painting of a detailed depiction of one of the battlefields from the American Civil War. Students silently wrote descriptions. Some made lists, while others wrote paragraphs. They wrote without stopping for four minutes.

Before showing the next slide, the teacher said, "I will now open the window pane so that the air gets into the room. Think about all five senses: sight, sound, smell, touch, and taste. Using the Freewrite strategy, you will now describe the scene using as many of the senses' references as possible." The next slide appeared. The picture is the same, except that there is a raised window pane to reflect that it's open.

Window Blinds Open
Describe what you see

Figure 9.3.   Window Activity

The students write, but unlike the Fastwrite, they pause frequently to think about their choice of words. Some continue to make lists or columns with each of the senses labeled at the top. Other students write in narrative form and incorporate the sensory details along the way. They write for eight minutes.

The teacher shows the final slide. There is only the picture with no window. The teacher says, "You are now transported out of the room and into the picture. You are part of the scene. Choose a person, item, or any other point of view, like a bird. Write as if you are that character in the middle of the scene. I encourage you to continue to use sensory details. You must at this point write in narrative form, as if you are there."

The students write for five minutes. Some use their lists to help them write. Others add to what they wrote in the previous round. Another group of students starts fresh narratives. All is quiet except for the tapping of keys and the scratching of paper.

When time is up, the teacher has students pair up. They read either their second or third piece of writing. After a couple of minutes, the teacher combines the pairs into quads, and repeats the process. Students talk animatedly.

Window Blinds Open
Describe what you see

Figure 9.4.   Window Activity

Window Opens
Describe the scene using senses other than sight (sound, smell, taste, touch)

Figure 9.5.   Window Activity

You enter through the window
Describe the experience with you as a participant

Figure 9.6. Window Activity

Analysis and Reflection

The Window Activity is a writing approach that helps students develop skills in composing details. It is also a confidence builder for the many students who lack confidence in their writing. The structure of the Window Activity uses an image with lots of details as a focal point for students to unpack. When running out of ideas, the student looks at a different section of the picture for fresh details to add.

Encouraging students to make lists, columns, or paragraphs for the first two writing exercises supports the learner's approach to organizing information. Lists and columns allow students with weak writing skills, or low self-confidence, to focus on the task of finding details without the perceived writing skills getting in the way. The Fastwrite and Freewrite[5] strategies offer a mix of generating ideas for which at least one will suit each learner. For the final round of writing, the students choose their preference, having done both.

Finally, sharing their writing in pairs and quads is a way to listen to narratives by others, as well as hear their own as they read aloud. This added communication gives students the experience of hearing a variety of writing and the use of details in a nonjudgmental forum. Often, students who thought that they were poor writers, discover that they have more skills than they were able to recognize before.

TEACHING LEARNING PREFERENCES
THROUGH PROCESSES

Using learning preferences to help students process understanding is the one area in this chapter that a teacher has the greatest impact. Knowing students per the learning profile cards helps with grouping and personalizing instruction. There are whole class teaching practices that can raise or damage learning, when informed by how students process.

Example One: Wait Time and Think Time

After direct instruction, the teacher showed three clips of a video about environmental practices and impacts on animal habitats. After each four-minute clip, the teacher asked comprehension questions. She paused 5 to 15 seconds after asking a question, ignoring any raised hands. After the pause time, she called on students, not always choosing someone with their hand in the air.

Next, the teacher transitioned to the paired-verbal fluency protocol.[6] Students were paired off based on their nine o'clock partners.[7] Based on the previous content work about the topic, each pair took turns talking, while the other listened during two complete rounds, starting at 60 seconds and ending with 30 seconds each.

The teacher had the students reflect on the conversation and identify new insights and/or new learning. She gave them two minutes of think time, allowing them to journal or list ideas. At the end of the time, the teacher had students pair with their three o'clock partners to share. They then submitted their thoughts on a half sheet of paper, before moving on to the next phase of the lesson.

Analysis and Reflection

Wait time[8] and think time are methods for giving students sufficient time to think through their understanding of concepts before discussions or moving forward to new content. In "Using 'Think-Time' and 'Wait-Time' Skillfully in the Classroom,"[9] Robert J. Stahl states, "Students must have uninterrupted periods of time to process information, to reflect on what has been said, observed, or done, and to consider what their personal responses will be."

The teacher in the aforementioned example made a conscious effort to pause 5 to 15 seconds after asking each question. The intent was to give all students time to consider how to organize their thoughts around their answers. Studies done on wait time length have found that the average time a teacher pauses after asking a question, before calling on a student or answering the question themselves, is:

One second.

One second gives no opportunity for reflection or organizing one's thoughts. The high end of pause time was 1.5 seconds, which has no noticeable improvement. There are learners who feel unprepared to answer any questions unless they are given time to silently process the ideas for themselves. They are the people at meetings who say little at the start of a topic. Yet when they do speak up, their ideas tend to ring with clarity as if they have captured the main ideas or thoughts of the group. For purposes of this book, let's call them, internal thinkers. One second pause sets them up for frustration.

There are learners who tend to jump into a conversation, without perceived thoughtful contemplation. For them, dialogue is a means to shape understanding in the moment. Let's call them, external thinkers. Teachers tend to honor them as the ideal learner because they are ready to attempt answers to questions immediately, even if their ideas are partially formed at best.

By waiting 5 to 15 seconds, the teacher insists that all students take time to consider their ideas. This pause levels the playing field so that a teacher does not have to ask for volunteers, they can call on them.

Paired-verbal fluency is a way to help students practice listening skills and have think time to consider the ideas expressed, as there is no cross-talk allowed. Each student gets a block of time to talk or think, depending on who is in the speaker role and who is in the listener role. Doing multiple rounds tends to deepen the conversation. Students may refer to their notes and texts. The teacher uses think time for two minutes as a means to ask a question that requires more than state the facts. Placing value on new learning, students need more than 15 seconds, if the hope is for a thoughtful response.

The hardest part for using wait and think time is for the teacher to become comfortable with silence. Silence is often equated with nothing happening. Often time, silence is a good opportunity for practicing reflection and cementing ideas before moving on to the next activity. It helps to determine which students are ready to tackle the class and homework assignments and who needs additional support if they are to maximize their success with such activities.

Example Two: Chip Boards and Virtual Boards

Jennifer Allan is a middle school teacher at A2 STEAM @ Northside Elementary School in Ann Arbor Public Schools, in Ann Arbor, Michigan. As a math and science teacher, her approach to students always includes differentiation. Chip Boards and Virtual Boards work well as interest-based differentiation.

Jennifer takes these strategies to a higher level by intentionally incorporating learning preferences. She states:

> When I teach my students to add and subtract integers, I use a variety of methods. We typically start with number lines, a visual model that helps students understand distances between numbers, a foundation that later leads to a deep understanding of the concept of absolute value. We then move on to chip boards, in which we use black chips to represent positive integers and red chips to represent negative integers.
>
> Students can easily see how positive and negative quantities balance each other (one red chip and one black chip is referred to as a "zero pair"). It allows them to clearly visualize how subtracting negative numbers increase the quantity, and how adding a negative number decreases the quantity, two particularly difficult concepts to grasp. My tactile learners adore using the chip boards; in fact, I often joke that the fastest way to find out who your tactile learners are is to put out some manipulatives and see which students make a beeline for them.
>
> Once all of the students have mastered the use of chip boards, I introduce a virtual option, using the National Library for Virtual Manipulatives.[10] Having offered my students a variety of tools for them to use, I now allow them to choose the tool that best suits their learning style. Offering different modalities for a given content area is not some flashy trick; it is instead a response to my clear responsibility as an educator to meet my students' needs.

Analysis and Reflection

Jennifer Allan's use of Chip Boards and Virtual Boards supports the sense-making process that learners need to do when digesting content. Such activities could be a way for introducing new concepts in a subject, or be the product work that students complete to demonstrate their learning. In this example, students receive ongoing experiences that enable them and their teacher to monitor growth and understanding. As students move from the physical chips to the virtual work, there are multiple opportunities to check for understanding, and gather the students needing additional support, while others proceed with the work.

Embedding the learning profiles, Jennifer Allan does not assign students to tasks. She incorporates learning modalities into the experiences and lets the students make their choices. She recognizes that the learner is the best judge for what appears to fit their thinking at that moment. If the choice turns out not to be effective, the student can take a different path. The options are in place.

TEACHING LEARNING PREFERENCES
THROUGH PRODUCTS

Products are an area for giving options that are infused with the way that students think about showing what they know. Learning styles or theories of multiple intelligences can be useful. When crafting product options, each choice should lead with at least one learning preference, with another one infused in the process.

Also note that in the following examples, students are not assigned a product based on their perceived learning preferences. They are expected to choose for themselves. Sometimes their choices will be surprising. It does not mean that their learning preference was not identified correctly. Interest always plays a role. Students may choose out of interest and deal with the subtle challenges of other learning preferences as a growth opportunity.

Example One: Sternberg Multiple Intelligences Activity

The students explored different persuasive elements through many lessons. They were now charged with composing a persuasive message for promoting a vacation destination. Digital media was required, but the tool used was up to the students. Using the differentiation lens of personalization through student voice, they were given three avenues for creating their persuasive message:

1. Create a logical case that promotes four key components of any good vacation destination.
2. Choose a location that a travel agent contact needs help promoting. Use some of their ideas in the promotion.
3. Choose a target demographic of vacationers and present based on what would appeal to them most.

The final products were posted on the classroom blog for public review and comments. Students chose the one that interested them the most. Some students could not decide, and asked the teacher for guidance. Based on their learning profile cards, the teacher steered them to the product option that might best match their approach to thinking. Ultimately, students decided which one they would do.

Analysis and Reflection

A Sternberg activity is based on the work by Robert Sternberg's triarchic theory of intelligence.[11] There are three intelligences to focus on:

- Analytical: Looking at concepts through abstract methods and explanations. This is often how content is taught in schools.
- Practical: Viewing concepts in context to real-world contexts in the community and/or through the lens of student interests. When students leave the classroom how might they see or use the learning in their personal lives?

• Creative: See concepts from different points of view or perspectives. It's like the ambassador or salesperson who tries to understand from the perspective of diplomats and clients so that they can better negotiate, or the inventor who sees a coffee cup and designs an innovative new design for travel. Students tackle new and innovative ways of explaining and analyzing concepts.

According to this theory, everyone has the capacity to be strong in all three areas. With a growth mind-set, one could develop their sense of perspective in all areas through practice. When a Sternberg activity is designed with three product options, students do not need to be assigned to any task. Allow them to choose the task that catches their interest the most. If they are stuck then they might be persuaded to a certain task based on how they best process information.

Example Two: Three-Dimensional Product Learning Preferences

Having taught lessons about fractions, it was time for the students to demonstrate what they understood regarding the parts and function of fractions. The teacher, Tamela Rinehart, chose to use the Think Dot activity, as described in the chapter, Differentiation through Readiness.[12] The experience was intended to be a formative practice opportunity by students. The teacher would use the results and her observations of the students to add supports to the lesson that followed the next day. As students roll the die, they completed the selected task.

Analysis and Reflection

Each box contains a task that represents a different learning preference component. The first box asks for a traditional abstract definition. The second box has students puzzle out the picture. The third requires a drawn representation. The fourth poses the challenge of crafting a word problem. The fifth and sixth focus on real-world experiences: pizza and test scores respectively.

Students experience the different approaches to fractions so that they can find some that are more comfortable than others. Having various learning preferences demonstrated does not by itself ensure learning will take place nor will they necessarily make the tasks more difficult. What it does is provide students the opportunity to see how the concept is applied and viewed from different perspectives. This can lead to some interesting conversations when students work in groups on the tasks. The design of two think dots for fractions was a way to also tier based on readiness.

This particular task has inspired other teachers to create their own versions.[13] Here is one by Sarah Brown, a math coach and teacher in Metro Nashville Public Schools:

Think Dots

Understanding Fractions (Tiered & Learning Profiles)

Instructions: Choose and complete 5 of the 6 tasks. Task 1 must be one of the choices. Show and explain all work.

What is the top of the fraction called? What is the bottom of the fraction called? ●	Write a fraction for the shaded area. ●● ●	Draw a picture that shows 2/3. ●● ●
Make a word problem that explains 7/10. ●● ●●	If you have 3/5 of a pizza eaten, what part is left? ●● ●● ●	If you had the following scores on a test, which would be better? $\dfrac{\text{Right}}{\text{Total}}$ $\dfrac{1}{2}$ or $\dfrac{4}{6}$ ●●● ●●● ●●●

Figure 9.7-1   Fractions: Learning Preferences and Readiness—Example One

Instructions: Complete 4 of the 6 tasks. Tasks 1 and 2 must be completed. Show and explain all work.

• What is the top # of the fraction called? • What is the bottom # of the fraction called? • What do these numbers represent? ●	Name 2 different fractions that could represent the picture.	Draw a picture that shows $$\frac{1+2}{3\ \ \ 3}$$
Make a word problem that explains 3/8	If 3/8 of the race is bicycling, 1/8 is swimming, how much of the race is left to run?	If you had the following scores on a test, which one would be better? $$\text{Right} \quad \frac{1}{2} \text{ or } \frac{4}{6}$$ $$\text{Total}$$

Figure 9.7-2

Think Dots

Fractions (Tiered 3)

Use the word bank to label the correct parts of a fraction: ¾	5/8	3/5
3 is the _____ and 4 is the _____. A fraction represents a _____ of a whole. Denominator, part, numerator ●	Shade in the correct fraction: ●●	Draw a picture to represent this fraction. ●●●
4/7 Complete the story problem. Sarah ate 4 _____ out of the _____. ●● ●●	Thomas ate 2/6 of the pizza. How much is left for the rest of the family? ●● ●●●	Which student did better on the test? Student A: 3/6 | X	X	☺
X	X	☺ | Student B: 5/8 | ☺	☺	☺
X	X	☺
X	X	| ●●● ●●●

Guiding Questions for planning:

Objective: What should students know and understand when this lesson is completed?

Assessment: How will students show what they learned or did not learn the objective after the activity is completed?

Activity: How does the Think Dot support the objective and prepare students for the assessment?

Figure 9.8. Fractions: Learning Preferences and Readiness—Example Two. List the lesson's objective and related assessment, before developing the Think Dots for best results. Editable doc at http://openingpaths.org/blog/resources/

FINAL THOUGHTS

What is important to remember about learning preferences is that learners should never be categorized as having one strength, nor be limited to a few areas that are deemed in their purview of understanding. Each person is complex, and no one is a robot. As demonstrated in this chapter, learning preferences help to inform and enhance learning experiences by providing multiple ways to explore one's thinking. Sometime a strategic approach is needed to personalize for someone who needs support in their growth, from learning disabilities to gifted and talented. Sometimes even these labels can be mixed.

Understanding how learners process information such as the internal and external thinkers should influence how teachers use instruction that honors both. Teachers can be intentional in what they ask of students to organize or process concepts through the 15 second pause for wait time and the 2- to 5-minutes think time. The key is a willingness by teachers to reflect on their own practice, identify their areas of comfort, and those learning approaches that do not fit their comfort zone. When teachers develop the latter area, they can influence more students.

INVITATIONS TO REFLECTION

As a result of this chapter, use the lens for differentiation to consider the following questions for a self-guided exploration of your practice and those whom you support.

1. Review the suggested strategies shared in this chapter for use in content, process, or product. Also find more strategies at www.SoAllCanLearn. org. How might you use one or two strategies to meet learner needs of all your students?
2. What are one or two problems with using learning preferences? What are the guides or solutions to avoid or overcome the problems?
3. Why do assessments play a key role in effective use of differentiation through learning preferences?
4. Why are process learning preferences approaches so little used despite its critical value?
5. How much influence does or should learning preferences have on activities that are based on readiness and/or interests?
6. What will be your next step for including, improving, or expanding differentiation through learning preferences in your work with students and colleagues?

Crossroad Planning Invitation

- Design or revise a learning activity that focuses on interest. Use one of the elements: content, process, and/or product as your focus.
- Facilitate a group or staff dialogue about learning preferences. Generate a list of 20+ strategies or ways to differentiate existing strategies based on learning preferences.

Enrichment Option

While completing the aforementioned task, include one or more of the following, as referenced throughout the book:

- Student Voice
- Formative assessment cycle
- Three-dimensional instruction frame

NOTES

1. John Hattie and Gregory Yates. *Visible Learning and the Science for How We Learn.* Routledge. 2013.

2. John Hattie's list for expert teachers is found on pages 107–108.

3. For a summary lesson outline go to www.SoAllCanLearn.org.

4. The Window Activity was first introduced to me by Sally Jessup in 2000. A great teacher of writing and coach, she shared how her design impacted students to build confidence in their writing. The Window Activity also has many benefits from a differentiation perspective.

5. Fastwrite and Freewrite are very useful strategies. When combined, they have an even larger impact. For more details find an article through www.SoAllCanLearn.org.

6. Paired-verbal fluency helps students practice listening and reflection skills. It makes for a good process tool and formative assessment of learning.

7. Clock Partners is a management strategy. Each marking period, students sign up with 12 peers to become partners if their common number is called. Find more information at www.SoAllCanLearn.org.

8. Wait Time was first introduced by Mary Budd Rowe in 1972. Her research found that such time tended to not exceed 1.5 seconds, but saw improvement by just pausing three seconds. In this chapter, 5 to 15 seconds is recommended depending on the complexity of the answers expected of students.

9. Robert J. Stahl. Using "Think-Time" and "Wait-Time" Skillfully in the Classroom, ERIC Publications, http://eric.ed.gov/?id=ED370885, Full Text: http://files.eric.ed.gov/fulltext/ED370885.pdf.

10. National Library for Virtual Manipulatives can be found at http://http://nlvm.usu.edu/ along with other links at www.SoAllCanLearn.org.

11. Robert Sternberg's triarchic theory of intelligences

"What Does It Mean to Be Smart?" Educational Leadership. March 1997. http://www.ascd.org/publications/educational-leadership/mar97/vol54/num06/What-Does-It-Mean-to-Be-Smart%C2%A2.aspx.

"Recognizing Neglected Strengths" Educational Leadership. September 2006. http://www.ascd.org/publications/educational-leadership/sept06/vol64/num01/Recognizing-Neglected-Strengths.aspx.

"Allowing for Thinking Styles" Educational Leadership. November 1994. http://www.ascd.org/publications/educational-leadership/nov94/vol52/num03/Allowing-for-Thinking-Styles.aspx.

12. Think Dots has many uses under a variety of conditions. A good Think Dot construction will include readiness, interests, and learning preferences.

13. A template for making your own Think Dots is available at www.SoAllCan Learn.org.

Appendix I: Differentiation and Research

In elementary classrooms across the country, teachers use guided reading[1] to work with students to improve their reading skills. Many teachers follow a process based on assessment data regarding reading decoding and comprehension skills. Students are placed into groups, who share common needs. Each group receives specific coaching and instruction around common readings so as to improve their reading level.

A cycle of formative assessments is used for checks and diagnosis of needs. The groups are fluid, which means that students are moved to the group that best addresses their needs. Learners can relocate to higher or lower reading level groups as needed. This is better than a past practice where students found themselves in a reading group as a year-long sentence. There were the bluebirds, the red birds, and the yellow birds. Everyone knew which group were the buzzards.

Guided reading is widely used as a staple part of improving reading skills. By its inherent structure, differentiation is an integral part of the electricity, like the human nerve system, that makes the system successful.

Response to Intervention (RtI)[2] is another research-based system used in many schools K-12. In this approach, staff look at student data to identify groups of students with specific support needs for core skills in such areas as literacy and numeracy. Teams review the data for general education students to identify the kinds and levels of interventions needed so that identified students receive the support needed to close their achievement gap. Like guided reading, RtI requires differentiation to fully execute meeting the various needs of students as identified and diagnosed for each learner. Differentiation is a critical lens on practice and learning that is integral to both systems, which are research-based approaches.

Unfortunately, when people ask genuine questions about the research that demonstrates the effectiveness of differentiation, they look at the lens as separate from the many research-based practices and systems. To say that differentiation is not research-based and, therefore, should not be used to meet the needs of diverse learners, tend to not argue against the needs of students in Special Education and Gifted Education. By the nature of these two support organizations for different ends of the spectrum, differentiation happens. And if there are different needs for Special Education and GATE, then the diverse needs of those in between cannot be ignored.

THE DIFFERENTIATION LENS

Differentiation is a lens for having a proactive impact on learning through collecting and using assessment data to inform instruction for groups and individuals. Educators are the best for understanding and explaining the inner workings of differentiation, making what is hazy to most—become clear.

It is the charge of educators to provide concrete explanations of successful strategies that incorporate the lens for differentiation, so that colleagues, both critics and those who hunger to understand, can see.

There are districts and governmental organizations that tell classroom teachers that they may only use strategies and systems that are proven through research. A challenge is when educators have tunnel vision for following these approaches, instead of being innovative and adapting the strategies based on their students' needs. Others sometimes feel limited from exploring different ways of instruction and learning that might have an impact, because the course of action has not yet been proven. This chicken or egg scenario slows progress and creates a culture of mistrust for teachers' capacity to innovate.

FINDING SOLUTIONS

A solution is to innovate from within so as to eventually push beyond such artificial barriers. Any proven strategy or system can be differentiated. This includes ones that are backed by research as effective. Consider restorative practices.[3] The system teaches students and adults how to communicate and resolve issues, such as dissolving resentments and raising awareness about how one's actions have a ripple effect on others, like the result of dropping a stone in a pond. The system leads to improved relationships among students and with teachers, which can make the learning environment a better place. When students feel that their voice is heard about important issues of school culture and relationships, consider how their voice plays into classroom instruction and learning.

When teachers have a deeper understanding of their students through restorative practices, how might that impact the conversations that take place for learners who struggle with understanding and other learners who feel bored by what they consider content already known? Good teachers will *see* students more fully and use intuitive differentiation to meet learners' needs, and inform their preplanning of crossroad lessons. Great teachers will use the same lens while planning instruction so as to personalize instruction for students who need the extra energy to lift them forward.

Guidelines for Differentiating Research-Based Strategies

Teachers can use the differentiation lens to pilot or scout innovative approaches to instructional practices and strategies, not just systems. The key to differentiating is to ensure that the experiences and structures align with the learning outcome(s). Follow this suggested guideline for successful implementation:

1. What are the learning outcomes: skills and concepts?
   What do learners need to know, understand, and apply? Sometimes such outcomes need to be unpacked to identify the components, which helps for building better supports for comprehension and application levels.
2. How might learners demonstrate what they can do: skills and concepts?
   This step is about designing a *draft* of the assessment for having an understanding how students might show what they know and do not know. When differentiating, the assessment is in draft mode so that its design can be personalized where needed, depending on the learners. Such changes or adaptations is one area of differentiating while staying true to the learning outcomes.
3. How does a review of learner data inform our lesson frame?
   Differentiation should always be intentional and specific to a need during pre planning. Learner data tells what students know, their gaps, and needs to fill-in the gaps. When an instructional practice is a force fit for learners, the usual reason is that teacher comfort level took precedence over student needs. A strategy that is research-based may not fit what your particular group of students need. Either modify it—be innovative—so there is a match to the learner, or set aside and choose a research-based approach that is better suited.
   What is the best placement of the strategy—content, process, and/or product?
   This is done in concert with 3A. Understanding learner data helps identify where in the lesson—content, process, and/or product—is best

to differentiate whole class, small groups, and/or individually. It's separated here because of the importance to simultaneously think about student data and where its application is most beneficial for improved learning during the lesson.

4. How are learners engaged and invited into doing the activity: readiness, interests, and/or learning preferences?

Learners, of all ages, make choices as to what they will spend time doing. Consider yourself as a learner. What conditions for support and challenge (readiness), relevance to work or life (interests), and modes of delivery and processing (learning preferences) are needed to encourage your choosing to participate? The same is true of classroom students. If they are not robots to be programed or buckets that passively wait to be filled, then effective teaching takes place when readiness, interests, and learning preferences needs are incorporated into instruction.

When using differentiation as a lens for instructional planning for learning, any practice, strategy, and system can be adjusted, adapted, or changed for meeting instructional needs. Whether the support is customized to the group or personalized to students, absolutely any approach can be differentiated. Obviously, poor instructional practices that fail to adequately meet learner needs, when differentiated will likely provide little or no gains for the student. Instructional practices that help students can be differentiated to further enhance and grow learning experiences.

Example in Practice #1

RAFTs is a good example of a writing strategy that helps students improve author craft regarding audience and communication focus. As explained in Chapter 7, students take on a role as a point of view. The students need to construct their message for the audience. The format is the form of the communication, such as a letter, speech, proposal, script, or poster. The topic is the focus of the communication, which should include a strong verb to engage students in a call to action. Here is an example of a typical RAFTs. It has not been differentiated.

RAFTs is a good strategy that helps teach the context for writing. What if the single option is one that students either do not understand or find boring? Here is a simple adaptation to improve the experience. Offer several choices, which differentiate through interests.

The first two choices are standard teacher-generated options. The third choice has blanks that the student gets to fill in based on their interest. The fourth choice is completely open to the students to construct a RAFTs of their own. The proposed RAFTs must be approved by the teacher, but the heavy lifting of design is laid on the student's shoulders.

Example in Practice #2

Another example is using the work from *Classroom Instruction That Works* (ASCD).[4] This book looked at instructional approaches that have the greatest impact on learning based on the authors' meta-analysis of research. As a result of their extensive work, they proposed ideas from McREL, the Essential Nine[5] instructional approaches.

1. Identifying similarities and differences
2. Summarizing and note taking
3. Reinforcing effort and providing recognition
4. Homework and practice
5. Nonlinguistic representations
6. Cooperative learning
7. Setting objectives and providing feedback
8. Generating and testing hypotheses
9. Cues, questions, and advance organizers

These approaches have research that supports them as having a significant effect on learning when used. For each chapter, the authors provide the research studies done on the particular instructional approach, including the effect size of the impact for learning. In each case, the effect size is significant.

The research that supports these approaches, or the book written about them, *Classroom Instruction That Works* (ASCD), does not include

Popular Sovereignty: principle that the people are the source of all governmental power

Objective: Explain how the principle of popular sovereignty limits the powers of federal government as reflected in the Constitution.

GLCE: 4-C2.0.1
Explain how the principles of popular sovereignty, rule of law, checks and balances, separation of powers, and individual rights (e.g., freedom of religion, freedom of expression, freedom of press) serve to limit the powers of the federal government as reflected in the Constitution and Bill of Rights.

Assessment: Exit card—What is Popular Sovereignty? Explain what it should mean to Americans regarding our government.

RAFTS Activity
Read the article then argue your view of popular sovereignty using the topic below. Include two to three supporting ideas.

Role	Audience	Format	Topic + Strong Verb
Newly naturalized citizen	Senator	Outline or Concept Map	Represent me or I can vote you out of office.

Figure A.1.   RAFTs: Non-Differentiated Version

The Text of the Constitution, Preamble

We the People of the United States, in Order to form a more perfect Union, establish Justice, insure domestic Tranquility, provide for the common defense, promote the general Welfare, and secure the Blessings of Liberty to ourselves and our Posterity, do ordain and establish this Constitution for the United States of America.

As explained in The Words We Live By by Linda Monk

> "The adoption of the Constitution was...the most participatory, majoritarian, and populist event the Earth had ever seen."
> ——Akhil Reed Amar, Yale Law Professor

These first three words of the Constitution are the most important. They clearly state that the people—not the king, not the legislature, not the courts—are the true rulers in American government. This principle is known as popular sovereignty.

But who are "We the People"? This question troubled the nation for centuries. As Lucy Stone, one of America's first advocates for women's rights, asked in 1853: "'We the People'? Which 'We the People'? The women were not included." Neither were white males who did not own property, American Indians, or African Americans—slave or free. Justice Thurgood Marshall, the first African American on the Supreme Court, described this limitation:

For a sense of the evolving nature of the Constitution, we need look no further than the first three words of the document's preamble: 'We the People.' When the founding fathers used this phrase in 1787, they did not have in mind the majority of America's citizens....

The men who gathered in Philadelphia in 1787 could not...have imagined, nor would they have accepted, that the document they were drafting would one day be construed by a Supreme Court to which had been appointed a woman and the descendant of an African slave.

Through the amendment process, more and more Americans were eventually included in the Constitution's definition of "We the People." After the Civil War, the Thirteenth Amendment ended slavery, the Fourteenth Amendment gave African Americans citizenship, and the Fifteenth Amendment gave black men the vote. In 1920, the Nineteenth Amendment gave women the right to vote nationwide, and in 1971, the Twenty-sixth Amendment extended suffrage to eighteen-year-olds.

http://www.constitutioncenter.org/constitution/details_explanation.php?link=004&const=00_pre_00&active=explain&searchlink=

differentiation in the list. But using the lens for differentiation reveals the influences that exist. Teachers who intentionally plan with differentiation in mind can use these research-based instructional approaches to construct learning experiences that meets the needs of all of their students. Here are some examples:

1. IDENTIFYING SIMILARITIES AND DIFFERENCES

Graphic organizers and certain thinking maps are means to structure a learner's thinking, such as a Venn diagram or comparison matrix. Group students

Popular Sovereignty: principle that the people are the source of all governmental power

RAFTS Activity
Read the article then argue your view of popular sovereignty using one of the topics below.
Include two to three supporting ideas.

Role	Audience	Format	Topic + Strong Verb
Newly naturalized citizen	Senator	Outline or concept map	Represent me or I can vote you out of office.
16-year-old Harvard scholar	Congress person	Op Ed	Give me the vote. I have a constitutional right to be heard.
Choose an elected official:	The people		I am powerful, so long as you let me.
Open Choice	Open Choice	Open Choice	Open Choice

based on their readiness skill level and give them the graphic organizer that supports their processing. Also, consider the complexity of the content that each group uses for identifying similarities and differences. Sometimes, the variation may be that the preloading of information in the organizer as a support for those who may benefit, helping them focus on the important items. For grouping based on mixed-skill levels, consider content that connects with shared interests so that participating students have real-world context for the content that they are comparing or classifying.

2. SUMMARIZING AND NOTE TAKING

Use oral or written summaries, or a combination via Think-Pair-Write. Try different protocols for reflection and dialogue that are mentioned in the various chapters of this book, such as Paired Verbal Fluency, Save the Last Word, Say Something, Literature Circles, and Affinity Mapping. Craft images or diagrams (nonlinguistic representations) that capture the key ideas. Teach two to three forms of note taking, and allow students to choose the one they prefer.

3. REINFORCING EFFORT AND PROVIDING RECOGNITION

Based on use of learning profile cards, discussed in Chapter 9, identify how students rate themselves on capacity to succeed in the course and related skills. Use this information for ongoing reflection on their progress. One way is to maintain learning portfolios that students use to reflect on their growth based on academic criteria. Also, use growth mind-set language to encourage students via their achievements and growth (Chapter 6).

4. HOMEWORK AND PRACTICE

Provide purposeful practice as homework that addresses specific needs of students for academic growth. Homework can be tiered, customized to each student's skill level needs. Other times, interests can be the way that students relate to the work and find meaning. It's important that the purpose of the homework is for practice and not assessment.[6] Practice sends the message that errors in the work are expected and will be used to develop appropriate supports that respect the needs of all learners.

5. NONLINGUISTIC REPRESENTATIONS

Use a combination of images and words, such as with Frayer Model and chunking videos with questions via Zaption.com and www.Edpuzzle.com. There are many digital tools that can help support student learning through nonlinguistic representations, such as Piktochart.com.[7]

6. COOPERATIVE LEARNING

Learning profile cards helps to form thoughtful groups where every student can contribute to the learning activities based on their skills in such areas as academic and thinking styles. Use other strategies such as forming norms, Clock and Elbow Partners, Say Something, Save the Last Word for Me, and Fishbowl.[8]

7. SETTING OBJECTIVES AND PROVIDING FEEDBACK

Keeping the end in mind and communicating them to students gives learners the big picture of what they are working toward. Sometimes the objectives vary if a tiered activity is used where students are placed in groups based on skill level. In differentiation, if the objectives are different, they are related as building blocks to the main objectives. Some students work on basic skills that will lead them to the target objective. Others work on tasks that extend and deepen the learning outcome.

Feedback strategies can be differentiated in nature through small group and individual supports. The emphasis of feedback is that it is constructive, positive, and specific.[9] Effective instructional approaches include: Need to Know activity, KWL, Student-led Feedback groups, and Gallery Walks.

8. GENERATING AND TESTING HYPOTHESES

Work in cooperative or collaborative groups. Use learning profile cards to ensure that the groups have a mix of learning preferences for the possibility of different takes on the work. Use explore labs, scenarios, and case studies that are tiered to different readiness groups of students. Set up learning centers or stations that are either interests-based or structured around readiness, depending on the learners' needs.

9. CUES, QUESTIONS, AND ADVANCE ORGANIZERS

Use a variety of advance organizers, or provide an advance organizer prefilled to different levels based on the needs of students. Coach students on the Question Formulation Technique[10] to develop their questioning skills. Practice both "wait" time and "think" time (Chapter 9) so as to empower students to lead the learning experiences.

FINAL THOUGHTS

There is much literature on differentiated instruction that provides much about theories, testimonies, and anecdotal support of differentiation. Prominent researchers and educators have spent years exploring and improving understanding of the pedagogical practices that make up what is commonly called differentiated instruction. Teachers across the world see the differences in their learners. Yet, there remains skepticism.

Critics argue that there is little research that supports differentiated instruction as instructional practice. Some question its validity, calling for the data that shows strong support. The problem with the critics, and for some of the well-intended supporters, is that their focus on differentiated instruction leaves them blind to the many examples that surround them.

Practices and systems like those mentioned, guided reading and response to intervention are inherently fueled by differentiation. They look at student data to make informed decisions about how best to meet the needs of each learner. The What Works Clearinghouse, http://ies.ed.gov/ncee/wwc/, is a repository of many practices that are supported by research. There is much to mine for use. Some will have differentiation as an inherent part of its framework. Others, like the Essential Nine, can be adapted through differentiation for richer support so that all can learn.[11]

INVITATIONS TO REFLECTION

As a result of this chapter, use the lens for differentiation to consider the following questions for a self-guided exploration of your practice and those whom you support.

1. Why is learning assessments critical to effective learning experiences? How does this idea relate to Differentiation?

2. Using one of the Essential Nine, what might be two or more ways to adapt the practice for differentiation support?
3. In some research studies, a practice is found to lack sufficient evidence due to a lack of quality implementation. Why is it important to build teacher capacity of a practice before conducting a study? What other reasons might there be for lack of quality implementation?
4. Based on the research-based practices in the What Works Clearinghouse, http://ies.ed.gov/ncee/wwc/, choose an approved strategy or practice. Explain how it either embeds differentiation in its structure, or how using the differentiation lens it could be adapted for diverse learners.
5. What are ways that differentiation in a learning experience can be made visible to parents or other stakeholders?

Crossroad Planning Invitation

• Using differentiation, design or revise a learning experience using a research-based approach. Use as a focus: readiness, interests, and/or learning preferences.
• Facilitate a group or staff dialogue regarding three ways to differentiate a school or district mandated initiative that is research-based.

Enrichment Option

Make adaptations to a learning experience based on differentiating among *one homogenous group*, such as gifted and talented or low performing.

NOTES

1. Guided reading research:

   • Guided reading in the Balanced Reading Program by Melissa J. Rickey, Ed.D., http://education.jhu.edu/PD/newhorizons/strategies/topics/literacy/articles/guidedreadinginthebalancedreadingprogram/.
   • TEMP: Article: Fountas and Pinnell—Early Literacy Experts Offer New Reading Intervention Program http://www.openeducation.net/2009/05/15/fountas-and-pinnell-early-literacy-experts-offer-new-reading-intervention-program/.

2. Response to Intervention.

   • RTI Action Network. "What Is RTI." http://www.rtinetwork.org/learn/what/whatisrti.
   • RTI Action Network. "Tiered Instruction and Intervention in a Response-to-Intervention Model." http://www.rtinetwork.org/essential/tieredinstruction/tiered-instruction-and-intervention-rti-model.

- Susan Demirsky Allan and Yvonne L. Goddard. *Differentiated Instruction and RTI: A Natural Fit*. Education Leadership. ASCD. http://www.ascd.org/publi cations/educational-leadership/oct10/vol68/num02/Differentiated-Instruc- tion-and-RTI@-A-Natural-Fit.aspx.

3. Restorative Practices research:
From SafeSanerSchools.org: http://www.safersanerschools.org/evidence-effec tiveness/.

- Improving school climate: Evidence from schools implementing restorative practices (2014). http://www.iirp.edu/pdf/ImprovingSchoolClimate.pdf.
- Findings from schools implementing restorative practices (2009). http:// www.iirp.edu/pdf/IIRP-Improving-School-Climate-2009.pdf.The Promise of Restorative Practices to Transform Teacher-Student Relationships and Achieve Equity in School Discipline http://www.tandfonline.com/doi/abs/ 10.1080/10474412.2014.929950.

4. *Classroom Instruction That Works*, 2nd Edition. http://www.ascd.org/publica tions/books/classroom-instruction-that-works.aspx.
5. Essential Nine
Laura Varlas. *Getting Acquainted with the Essential Nine*. ASCD Express. 2002. http://www.ascd.org/publications/curriculum-update/winter2002/Getting- Acquainted-with-the-Essential-Nine.aspx.
6. Homework is topic of intense debate as to its value and purpose. Here are two articles that look at the topic from a focus on differentiated needs:
John McCarthy. Homework Balance, Part I. http://openingpaths.org/blog/ 2013/10/homework-balance/.
John McCarthy. Homework Balance, Part II. http://openingpaths.org/blog/ 2013/10/homework-balance-pt2/.
7. There are many digital tools that will support this and the other Essential Nine instructional approaches. 100+ Tools for Differentiating Instruction through Social Media. http://www.edutopia.org/blog/differentiated-instruction-social-media- tools-john-mccarthy.
8. The National School Reform Faculty www.nsrfharmony.org and www.Team pedia.net are good sources for protocols and team builders respectively to support the coaching of cooperation and its advanced cousin: collaboration.
9. Feedback is important toward learning. Here are two articles that provide insight in the personalized approach one can take with feedback that supports Student Voices.

- Grant Wiggins. Seven Keys to Effective Feedback. http://www.ascd.org/publi cations/educational-leadership/sept12/vol70/num01/Seven-Keys-to-Effec tive-Feedback.aspx.
- Jan Chappuis. "How Am I Doing?" http://www.ascd.org/publications/edu cational-leadership/sept12/vol70/num01/%C2%A3How-Am-I-Doing% C2%A2%C2%A3.aspx.

10. The question formulation technique is helpful for developing core skills in students asking questions, reflection, and inquiry.

- The Right Question Institute. http://rightquestion.org/education/.
- Dan Rothstein and Luz Santana. *The Right Questions*. http://www.ascd.org/publications/educational-leadership/oct14/vol72/num02/The-Right-Questions.aspx.

11. Find more resources and references at www.SoAllCanLearn.org.

Appendix II: The EdCamp Experience: Where Voice and Choice Matter

> We want to do something that is cross-curricular that all the 5th grade teachers [on this campus] can participate in. We want to try something new where students truly have a voice in how they learn.

Kathy Austrian, 5th grade teacher at Serene Hills Elementary in Lake Travis ISD, made this statement while I met with her and teammate Amanda Reedy. Both have been part of our NextGen program this year—a program that gives support to teachers willing to try new strategies in their classrooms. I am the instructional coach that worked with them. Neither had any idea what to do to bring this to fruition . . . nor did I.

An online article describing a teacher who had done an EdCamp in his classroom provided inspiration (Seliskar, 2014). Although we agreed that this idea could work, we also knew we needed more structure. The 5th grade class had almost 180 students and 7 teachers. What would EdCamp look like when implemented on this scale?

Kathy and Amanda began to raise awareness with their team about the concept of EdCamp. All the teachers were receptive, but the vision of how to implement this on a daily basis over a two-week period was still unclear; successful execution rested on Kathy and Amanda bringing it into focus. They started with a definition of and reasons for providing an EdCamp experience for students; then, they developed a theme ("Share Your Passion") and a driving question ("How Will You Inspire Others?"). To provide consistency among the seven classrooms, they clearly outlined daily activities with period by period instructions, video links, questions, and major points. They acknowledged that, as the process evolved, changes would likely occur, and they remained open to suggestions from their teammates regarding design, potential problems, and possible solutions.

Setting the stage for the students was a priority. Day 1, students arrived to butcher-papered hallways proclaiming, "What do you want to learn? Bring your passion! Bring your voice!" Students brainstormed topics they would like to learn about, writing on sticky notes and posting on the butcher paper. The hallway on Day 2 boasted the caption, "What will you teach? How will you inspire? Share your passion!" Students learned about different personality types and identifying strengths. This again led to discussions about passions, why people have different ones, and how to pursue them.

The remaining days leading to EdCamp included a variety of learning experiences. Students wrote proposals that included learning outcomes, identified materials needed (technology, props, etc.), and outlined presentations with time limits for each section. They learned about asking questions that prompt higher-order thinking and about facilitating discussion. They also practiced some classroom management skills to regain the attention of their audience, if needed. In the two days prior to EdCamp, students had the opportunity to practice their presentations, receiving feedback from the teacher and students in their classroom.

Throughout this time, Kathy and Amanda continued to provide daily agendas. With help from their team, they organized the sessions, reserved classrooms, and prepared sign-up sheets. There would be 85 presentations—85 shared passions—in 10 classrooms. Sessions were color-coded according to category (technology, arts and crafts, etc.) and enrollment in each was limited to 20 students so that all would have attendees. Students eagerly awaited the day before EdCamp when they would be able to sign up for the nine 15-minute sessions they would attend.

The day of EdCamp arrived, and a banner proclaiming, "edcamp—Where Voice and Choice Matter" greeted the excited students. Young presenters shared passions such as Creating Harry Potter Potions, Mysteries of the Deep, Channeling Your Inner YouTube, Advanced Bicycles, Bonjour-Learn about France, Tricky to Please-Architecture and Design, Flippin' Fun Gymnastics, Flowering Photography, Personal Finance and Business, Oncology, The Cupcake Fanatic, 3-D Printing, Acting with a Twist, and many other topics. Quiet students came alive when talking about their passions. Inclusion students shared their passions and received high praise from their peers. Students learned about themselves and others, about interests and strengths that were previously unrecognized. Teachers were simultaneously exhausted and exhilarated. Students were given voice and choice—and it was incredible.

EdCamp was a concept that started small, just a couple of teachers wanting to do something out of the ordinary. It spread to a team of teachers who were willing to trust each other and take a risk for their students. It further encompassed 180 normal students, transforming them into enthusiastic learners/

presenters who flourished in the freedom to study and share their passions. For all involved, EdCamp provided an extraordinary learning experience.

Published article at: http://openingpaths.org/blog/2016/09/edcampexperi ence/.

Cathy Hill
Lake Travis Independent School District

REFERENCE

Seliskar, Jason. 2014, January 9. "An Elementary Edcamp—An Unconference for Students." *Getting Smart*. Retrieved from http://gettingsmart.com/2014/01/element ary-edcamp/.

About the Author

John McCarthy, Ed.S., is an advocate for student voice in their learning his entire career. He started out as a high school classroom teacher, working in several schools of different social and economic conditions. He continued work as a school improvement consultant for Wayne County, Michigan, serving 35 school districts and numerous public charter schools, and is also an adjunct professor. He now consults and coaches school across the United States and internationally on differentiation and other instructional approaches.

John supports school cultures on improving teacher and learner capacity with instructional practices, including differentiation, personalization, blended learning, project-based learning, authentic learning experiences, formative assessment practices, and instructional use of technology. John writes articles regularly for various education publications that are widely shared by educators to educators.

Over the years, John successfully helps teachers and administrators find the capacity and talent within themselves to design and implement structures that benefit students taking more ownership of their learning. He helps them connect pedagogical concepts into practical skill sets for successful implementation. He works with schools across the United States, Australia, and Asia.